MW01518577

May you be bolder
with every tomorrow!

-elise

ELISE RUSSELL

BEHAVE
BOLDLY

YOUR DREAMS WON'T CHASE THEMSELVES

ISBN 978-1-7772342-0-1 (hardcover)
ISBN 978-1-7772342-1-8 (ebook)

ponyfriday.com   @ponyfriday

To your dreams.
May you have the courage to chase them.

THE
INTRO

You Might Have It in You

Behaving boldly isn't for everyone, but I was tired of telling my gut to shut up so I decided to play a different game—and I'm happier for it. I ditched the settle-for-less culture I was entangled in, gave the nine-to-five the middle finger and went out on my own as a creative entrepreneur to push boundaries, fail and try to stay nimble. The path to your dreams is hidden behind the façade of what you're supposed to do, and my story is still unfolding.

I want to read about how a quest gets started while it's fresh in the writer's mind. Not when it's decades in the past and so far from their current reality that they aren't even the same person anymore. Famous creatives seem out of reach. Their memories need to have cobwebs dusted from them to be told, and reading vague recollections doesn't satisfy me. I crave stories about people in the thick of their struggles.

So this is my first seven-ish years as an entrepreneur growing Pony Friday. It's my before-double-digits era, a time capsule of the years nobody ever talks about until they make it big and write their "remember when" book. This is how hard it is for me *today*, not how hard it *was*. This is a snapshot—the insider scoop I needed seven years ago. I'm sharing what's been possible in my journey in the hopes that the ways I've stood up and fought for my dreams might help you feel brave enough to do the same for yours. The fight is not always pretty (or even ever pretty at all), but it's always worth it.

> ## EMBRACE A MESSIER EXISTENCE

It may seem like I'm killing it because I have a book and stuff. Not so. I squirmed my way in here and simply refused to leave. I wasn't invited. If I'd waited to get an invitation to the things that I wanted to do, my life would be dull and my heart would be black with despair. We all have to decide where we belong, then make it our business to get there.

No Sugar Coating and Candy Sprinkles

I'm not sharing my story because I've made millions, or because Pony Friday is a raging success. I'm not sitting on a high horse (ha ha) telling you how to be successful. I'm confessing my right-now status, to show you the positives of chasing your dreams even without the guarantee of any earth-shattering success. I don't have some bomb-proof plan that's proven to work. I'm not running ads about my seven-figure sales funnel and the steps you need to take to build yours. I simply think you should stick your neck out and embrace a messier existence—an existence that's your own. Quitting your day job is a high-stakes choice, and it can work if you're up for the adventure and willing to take the risk. People get laid off all the time; you'd just be proactive about shifting your career. I believe we were born to evolve and thrive, and by putting ourselves in a position for growth we're fertilizing that path.

What the Heck *Is* Pony Friday?

We're the behave boldly hub for dream-chasers. Pony Friday is an evolving creature, a dream come to life, a monster that needs to be fed—we describe it as a hybrid creative boutique and motivational lifestyle brand. The boutique represents our creative contract work, which in turn funds the growing lifestyle brand. Our goal is to build an inspiration support system, complete with motivational talks, galvanizing bootcamps, encouraging blogs and entertaining videos. Right now, I'm still transitioning away from helping people and businesses behave boldly with their marketing.

Pony Friday is a creative whim that got carried away. That's the simplest way to explain it. The idea for Pony Friday popped into my head unexpectedly. I dared to grow my own garden of creativity, and from within it sprouted a pony.

Before I redirected my life, I felt trapped and disillusioned. I had a "dream job" as a professional ad agency creative. I was getting paid and winning awards, but I hated the office culture and politics. I just wanted to hide in my cave and work from home. I wanted out in a bad way. I didn't know what I was stepping out to do, or that I would one day build a business that would grow beyond just me. I didn't even have a desk at home. I had a laptop, wireless and a kitchen table. All I knew on the day that I quit was that I didn't want to be at that agency, or at any agency. I forced myself to step away from what I knew I didn't want, so that I could figure out what I *did* want. I was opening up to my life.

Going places to do things you don't care about is ludicrous. I wanted to create my own reality and live my own life. I had no idea what that would look like, but I knew I needed to own it. I never once looked back at that agency. Leaving that job was one of the most freeing times of my life.

I'm motivated to spend my life cultivating a more fun and creative world. And I want to share my experiences of pulling myself out of the nine-to-five factory mindset. I want more people to colour outside the lines and create things beyond themselves. Creative misfits weren't meant to conform to a nine-to-five; they were meant to make the world a more vibrant place. To stay motivated, you have to keep putting one foot in front of the other. If you can't do that on your own, you'll be in trouble, fast. I hunt for my supper, and learning to hunt isn't easy. If you've ever been hunting for anything, you know that you can turn up empty for days, or even weeks. Think about antiquers or wildlife photographers. That one find or that perfect shot can take what feels like forever, and even after you've got it you need to move swiftly onward to the next.

I've learned that it's okay to say things that make others unhappy. I've slid into client meetings with a devilish grin on my face and stated, "I'm about to be very unpopular." I'm the kind of supplier who tells you what I think you need to hear, not what I think you want to hear—that's how I build trust. It also means that I work with a limited number of select clients. I imagine that most have had the urge to fire me after I've showcased brutal honesty. And that same honesty is what you'll get here: the unvarnished truth of what my experience has been, what I've learned and what I still struggle with.

Behaving boldly is about going after what seems to be your calling and not getting caught in the web of lies that tells you what you should be doing. The sensible path is not a bold path. Sometimes behaving boldly seems a lot like behaving stupidly. (I mean, I carry around a four-foot cut-out of a pony, easily caught by gusts of wind.) We have to be brave in the face of looking stupid, in the face of fear.

A life lived in fear is boring.

These are the first years.

Me and Pony.

1

SMALL DREAMS SUCK

Ready with Iceberg-Sized Cold Feet

I'm not ready. Or, at least, I thought I wasn't ready. Truth. Excuse. I convinced myself that my business needed more time to grow before I wrote about it. I mean, what would I have to say if I wrote it too early? I was in the habit of brushing off anyone who asked too many questions about my life, so how could I write a whole book? Coming up with excuses as to why I *couldn't* do it was easy. It took time for me to tire of those empty reasons and simply write this darn book.

You'll never be as ready as you think you should be. I never am. I started Pony Friday before I was ready. I started writing this book before I was ready. High-five to me! The most valuable message for you in these pages is this: "If she can do it, so can I." Please. Do.

If more of us put ourselves out there—making things and dreaming aloud—more of us will follow. Go create. Be determined. Be consistent. Be fierce. Be judged. And encourage others to do the same. I'm out here like a stray cat on the sidewalk looking for a belly rub. Do me a favour. Start before you're ready.

Hold Your Horses, I'm Not Ready

Shoving excuses out of the way is my first step toward getting anything done. I have a lifetime of excuses. Excuses for why I didn't, haven't and can't. I didn't get the best grades because the teacher didn't like me. I'm not married because nobody asked me. I can't do the splits because I'm not flexible. All the reasons, justifications, explanations, cover-ups, stalls and dodging that held this book back were chest deep and pudding thick. "I'm writing a book" sounds cool, and it's way easier to say than to do. My excuses gave me a comforting place to rest, and a tough place to move through. Excuses hold us back from being brave. Excuses make mirages of our fears, and they keep us captive.

STOP COMING UP WITH EXCUSES

These roadblocks are sneaky and come in all shapes and sizes, but they're all lies. They're restrictive and take up more room than they're entitled to.

- There's literally no time.
- I don't have money for that.
- My bandwidth is maxed.
- There's no healthy food in the house.
- My house is too dog-hairy for visitors.
- Two dogs is one too many.
- It's too cold to walk the dogs.
- We can't camp in the rain.
- This is good enough.
- I can write later.

This is where behaving boldly comes in. It isn't an enchanted cloak that you don and suddenly your excuses vaporize and you're always killing it. I need to refresh my commitment to behaving boldly as often as I do my favourite social feed. (You know, that obsessive finger tug down your mobile screen to see what's new as of twenty seconds ago.) Choosing to be bold is something you have to do over and over and over again. It's a bit like sunscreen: you need to find the kind that works for you, apply it liberally before you run out to enjoy the rays, then put even more on after it soaks in. And you have to do it every time you want to go somewhere sunny or set your foot on a beach. Sometimes your go-to version of going for bold won't be enough to get you over the next big hump. Excuses, reasons and everyday life will always be there to trip you. Like that time you applied sunscreen like a good little soldier and still got burned.

I'll consistently pump out weekly blog post after weekly blog post, only to take an unplanned hiatus that lasts for months. What's that about? I get caught up in the idea that people get too many emails already and I have nothing of value to add—a kernel of truth and a touch of insecurity that bursts perfectly into an excuse like bit of fluffy popcorn. So my weekly blog becomes more of a once-in-a-certain-shade-of-blue-moon thing. I have amazing help, but it all boils down to me, and sometimes I fail at holding it all together. Maybe I set out to do more than I can handle. It happens. It's hard to know what you can handle until you exceed your limits and something ends up frozen and forgotten. The game then needs to shift to sort out what stays and what goes.

YOUR PRIORITIES DEFINE YOU

Take a good look at the things on your list, and decide what you need to keep and what you want to keep. If some have frostbite from being ignored, get back at them. It's easy to remember to feed and walk my dogs because they make a fuss, but when I stop putting out a blog, my readers might not even notice. Nobody holds me accountable except for me, because nobody cares the same way I do.

Your Excuses Are Boring

Have you ever noticed how eyes glaze over and friends stop listening when you talk about why you aren't doing something? We have to get out of our own way to stop being average. Repeated failure beats not trying. That said, I do recommend learning from mistakes. You'll have more than one chance, as long as you continue to *look* for more chances, so don't sweat that first leap. Give yourself another shot and don't expect it to go smoothly—that just sets you up for disappointment. And disappointment is crippling to progress.

SHATTER YOUR LIMITING BELIEFS

Still, as much as I know all of this, sometimes my mind goes back into a tailspin of excuses. Excuses can build walls as thick as a prison, and I have to be vigilant about not letting that happen. Self-made takes self-discipline.

If you're making excuses, saying you can't start chasing your dream today and you'll get to it in a couple of weeks, I want you to call bullshit on yourself. My forehead is scrunching up in pain at the thought of you not taking an action step right now. Toss this book aside. Your priorities define you.

Micro actions can feel trivial while you're doing them, but over time they add up to big results. Make your steps tiny enough to feel doable, and slot them in throughout your day. It's incredible how quickly things will start to take shape. I don't care if you can't find a solid hour to spare. Do you have a spare five or ten minutes freckled throughout your day? I do. How do you think I wrote this book? I didn't have a book deal, or a juicy budget that let me rent an apartment in France and not do anything for months except write and take walks in the countryside waiting for inspiration to strike. No. I fit it in the nooks and crannies.

I'm not perfect. This project was crammed into a random bin in a corner of my shelf for a year, doing nothing. The idea of completing this book scared the crap out of me, and I let it lurk around on my to-do list as a put-off chore. Draft one was a mutant waiting to be revised and I refused to touch it.

Hibernation Can Lead to Productivity

Hey, bread dough needs time to rise or it can't do its job. I wasn't ready to identify as an author. Sure, I've been a professional writer for years. An author, though? That seemed too momentous a leap, a height too high. Obviously, a writer can be an author, that's not even a half-step difference. I bet some of us even think of those two titles as the same thing. Writer. Author. Same-same. But I got nauseated at the thought of publishing literature with my name on it. The ridiculousness of this does not escape me. You have to shatter your own limiting beliefs. We bend and contort our fears in ways that sound absolutely absurd when spoken aloud.

It was once impossible for me to identify as a writer. I sometimes struggle to spell simple words. I once misspelled the word "skate" so awkwardly that I couldn't even search the correct spelling and had to ask someone. Homonyms are masterfully designed booby traps to trip me up. "Sheik" and "chic" aren't remotely in the same camp, but I succeeded in mixing them up. Oh, to have been a fly on the wall when my boss pointed out that bungle. I can't even with grammar. Subject. Verb. Object. I'm a grade schooler guessing at the difference. Throw in prepositions and my eyes roll back in my head.

REFUSE THE TRAP

Thankfully, I wrote anyway. My brain had come up with a mile-long list of reasons why I could not be a writer. But all I needed was one reason why I *could* be a writer. That's all you need: one reason to do something you thought you could not do. Just one. My excuses were just holding me back. I mix up words and make verbal blunders. So what? That just means I need to have sense of humour about it.

Take your time to diligently work through the shit that's holding you back; don't accept it as your reality. Never surrender to the asshole in your head who's telling you that you can't. Be strategic and play the long game to win.

Get Your Foot out of Your Grave

You haven't missed your window. The idea that opportunity is limited by age is crazy. Fuck age! There are countless examples throughout history of people overcoming odds and achieving things, whether they were young or old, with a house full of kids or without, with tons of debt or rolling in cash. It's a mindset. You decide if this is your time or not. If you're older, you have more life experience to pull from to be successful; you have more contacts; you have more failures you've learned from. You're more resilient. Younger people in theory have more time, but that's never guaranteed. Your window is waiting.

Easy for her to say, you might think. I'm over seven years in as I write this, and hindsight does make the act of quitting my job seem like it was effortless. I was thirty-three years old—younger, and more than a smidge naïve. If the idea of quitting had come to me later in life, I know I would have taken the same path at forty-three, fifty-three or sixty-three. What's crazy is to waste another minute doing something I'm no longer passionate about or inspired by. Yes, it can be tempting to fantasize about having started earlier, when you were younger and had your whole life ahead of you—but that's a waste of time. At twenty-three, I wouldn't have been ready for this type of responsibility and commitment. In my twenties, I was figuring out who I was and what I wanted. I needed to travel, explore new places and try on different versions of who I could be.

Living with a sensation of being behind on my accomplishments was part of my general emotional state for years. I always felt late. Our society can be great at making us all feel like under-accomplished assholes and ungrateful wastes of space. Life's joys always depend on what lens we view them through. And it's easy to view life through the lens of too late or not enough. In my thirties, I often felt like I was a lost creative who had missed the marriage boat and was never going to have children or check any of the other "necessary" life boxes to complete my lived-this-life-to-the-fullest list. That thought was often debilitating—it told me that I sucked at life.

We're in a trap. We're stuck trying to fight for our dreams against our own insecurities, while simultaneously having to fight for them against the societal standard of "how to live." It's too much. By all rational thinking, I should be on my second marriage with two kids in middle school who I fifty-fifty co-parent with another couple across town. Instead, I'm a never-married career creative and proud dog mom.

Refuse the trap. That's the only way I know to be grounded in my creativity and follow my instincts. I took myself to Paris for my thirtieth birthday and wandered around like a local. I adore simply being places and exploring the idea that I can have anything if I shift my mind enough to construct the complete assurance that it's mine. I'm not suggesting you can grow wings and fly if you simply put your mind to it, but who's to say you can't? Try things on with your imagination and see what's worth pursuing. Immerse yourself in your surroundings. Swaddle yourself in creativity. Bundle your world and embrace being an entrepreneur.

Quit Your "Dream" Job

In mere moments, I would be free. It was the start of a great summer. I could feel the liberty tickling my fingertips as I walked down the hall with my letter of resignation, ready to say what needed to be said. It was going to be amazing. I passed the freshly printed letter to the person who had recently been promoted after my boss had quit, the runner-up, and the person I had been avoiding reporting to.

Quitting has always been my favourite moment of any job. I'd been complaining for weeks, maybe months—okay, it was definitely years—about being stuck in the nine-to-five. And this time I was

Keep Lining Up the Right Pieces

> When my family does a puzzle together, we only get to look at the picture on the box once, then it's hidden away until the puzzle is complete. That's how it feels when I'm chasing my dream. Except it's more like I was out feeding the horses when everyone else got to look at the picture: I don't even know what my completed dream looks like.

quitting forever. This wasn't going to be another breakup-to-makeup scenario, or breakup-to-jump-back-into-another-agency-relationship-with-someone-just-like-you scenario, which had played out so many times in the past.

I'd quit agency life once before with the intention of leaving the nine-to-five for good, but a few months in I went through a relationship breakup and decided the boss move was to take over what was formerly a joint mortgage alone. I had needed my salary to manage the payments, but looking back, I can see that the timing still wasn't yet right to go out on my own. I was shaky in my conviction to renounce the herd hierarchy. Awards still meant a lot to me, and the idea of giving myself a title and printing that on my own business cards felt uncomfortable. The fight in me wasn't big enough yet.

You have to appreciate that I was a creative working in a creative department. That office even had air hockey and table tennis. Many places I'd worked had foosball tables and cool lounges with couches for us to brainstorm in. I had a dream job—it just wasn't my dream job.

It's worth reflecting back on how I ended up in a traditional nine-to-five job to start with. I've never enjoyed working in an office; it wasn't something I'd ever dreamed about. I never fantasized about the top-floor corner suite or the department that would report to me. I never coveted the parking spot or wanted to be a better version of my boss. Even weekends are hard to enjoy when you have to be back in that same office on Monday. I did what most sane people do when they find themselves in the circumstances of feeling stuck in their job. I looked for a different job.

DON'T SETTLE FOR ANY OLD DREAM JOB

I'm a bit embarrassed now by this narrow-minded thinking—I do call myself creative. But looking for a new job is logical, predictable and easy. (Why did my former self take so long to get on the behave boldly train? This is painful to remember. Ugh!) For talented creatives in good economies, there are plenty of places with openings, and I interviewed at a few of them to the point of turning down job offers.

I compare job hunting to trying on shoes. First, you hunt to see what styles are available, then you might try on a whole bunch of different models before you find ones that look great and fit just right. Sometimes you might even take them home, try them on with your favourite outfits and walk around the house in them before making the final decision. So that's what I did. I met creative department heads at coffee shops and restaurants, I went to agencies and met with several managers to establish that it would be a good fit, and then I realized they could never pay me enough. Predictable is bland. I need a certain amount of uncertainty and natural tension. There would never be enough money, vacation time or flex days in the world to keep me happy. I was over it.

At the beginning of any new relationship or job there's usually a bit of a head-in-the-clouds period. Everything is new, and new is exciting. There's nothing to complain about. You're learning what is and what isn't. You're absorbing information about people, projects and clients. You've got a new desk and fresh business cards. You tell everyone you've started a new thing and it's marvellous. Later, reality sets in.

I quit when I was on an award-winning streak doing great work. I was in the zone. Then the person I called my boss left to pursue other things and I was stuck reporting to someone else—someone dead-set on making changes and leaving their mark, changing the vibe and also the layout of the furniture to be more "integrated" and "team oriented" in the obnoxiously loud open-concept space. (Studies show that open-concept offices are terrible for productivity.) The successful creative space that I had carved out for myself, with my beautiful jungle of luscious plants, glass walls and a comfy over-stuffed yellow lounge chair for visitors was gone. I had the best spot around. It wasn't an office. It was an oasis. But it was being taken away.

A new toxicity crept in—as well as a no-shorts rule. What the heck? It was the middle of summer, I worked in a creative department, and they were starting to tell me what I could and could not wear to work. This place was wrecking my vibe.

First, I started working from home. Then I took the next step. "Here is my letter of resignation," I said, handing over my freshly printed ticket to a commitment-free summer. (I'm still not sure if using the office printer for a resignation letter is tacky or a boss move…) There is nothing quite as sweet as quitting. In my head I was jumping for joy and screaming *I quit! I quit! I quit!* Generally, putting on your most professional face is a necessity in these sorts of situations. I had not been happy. I'd brought it to the attention of the higher-ups more times than was appropriate. Quitting was my best option. It felt like fate, like destiny. It was my choice. It was a sign of better things—a porthole to freedom.

The summer was officially mine—and every month after. Over the next five years, I worked to establish Pony Friday, the only job I don't want to quit. With more autonomy, I found that my desire to create was renewed. I became a glowing light, a happy person, ready to dive in and produce imaginative wonder. I turned into a creative superhero. The more autonomy I have, the closer I get to my best. I sleep in when I need to, I walk the dogs in the mid-morning sun and I refuse to suffer through long meetings.

I need to know what I'm capable of doing, and I need room to make mistakes, and both of these things are great incentives to work for yourself. I wasn't meant to be a cog in a machine. Not being respected for my accomplishments is a total drag; when everyone else seems so happy with "good enough," fighting alone to be excellent is the pits. I had nothing to lose in quitting my agency job, and everything to gain.

But now that I'm making up my own rules, I have a different perspective. I left one game to play another. I used to be fighting for rank among others, now I'm fighting to matter at all. It's a bit weird. I quit. Now what? It's too hard, yet it's not *that* hard all at once—my brain flip-flops between being overwhelmed and feeling like I own this path.

Every Day Is Pony Friday

Pony Friday began as my nickname for Fridays off. It was the beginning of my slow migration away from the traditional working hours the world still plays by—you can't avoid the structure completely. I didn't just jump right in and have it all work out for me. I positioned myself for the serendipity of life, so things could slide into place at the right moment.

Before I decided to quit my job, an accountant friend of mine, with a nice cushy role at a major oil and gas firm, was about to get every Friday off all summer long. This accomplished woman also happened to have a horse. Instead of being envious, I decided to ask my employer if I could use up all my vacation days for the rest of the year to enjoy my own summer Fridays off. With their stamp of approval, I was off to the races, and my friend and I met to ride our horses together until we ran out of Fridays. It was brilliant.

SELF-LOVE ISN'T MEANT TO BE YOUR SIDE HUSTLE

It was everything I wanted a Friday to be and, to the annoyance of my friend, I referred to our time together as Pony Friday. I bet you can predict what happened next. Summer came to an end. Pony Fridays ran out, and I was back looking at an endless work schedule with no vacation time left. I could see that terrible moment coming. It looked bleak. And that's when I decided to quit my job and keep my Fridays free. They're still brilliant. And since I wanted my life to be the most fun possible, I started my own business and called it Pony Friday—a life I wouldn't need a vacation from.

Finding the One

Society puts so much pressure on us to couple up in a meaningful relationship. There is value in that, but it's important for you to have a deeper relationship with yourself too. You're saddled with you every minute of every day, so I recommend finding your dream and going after it. Self-love isn't meant to be a side hustle. Few of us would be interested in dating someone we can only see one Sunday a month.

I was thirty-four before I had any idea what people meant when they'd smile warmly and gush, "When you know, you know." Those people are smug assholes. What a vague and useless thing to say. I had no idea what that type of love felt like . . . until I did. Now, I get it, but it doesn't make those people any less smug.

I met the love of my life on a flight home from Boston. It was magical, the way everyone tells you it will be. The moment was unexpected. I'd been at a design conference with my friend and we were heading home. He appeared as we were getting settled into our seats before takeoff. My friend and I were going through our notebooks chatting about the people we'd met, the sessions we'd taken and the ones we missed. I'd seriously flirted with a couple of people, so we had a good laugh over that. Then, out of nowhere, there he was. He wasn't what I expected at all. I just saw him sitting there, and I knew it was meant to be. That's how it happened for me.

Introducing His Royal Highness, Pony

The idea of a sitting pony icon popped into my head. It was love at first sketch. That original sketch was so simplistic and ugly that it remained an idea for a year—but my gut told me it was important. Then I swear: Pony designed himself on my computer, and now he's taken on an entire life of his own. Other names were brainstormed for him, but nothing seemed more fitting than Pony. First name Pony, last name Friday! He's casual though, so you don't need to call him Mr. Friday or anything. Pony gets dressed in costumes and has his photo taken with people. He's evolved into something more than an icon for our brand, and he keeps pushing me to improve my game and keep showing up.

I fell in love with an idea. What I do for Pony is small compared to what he does for me. Every relationship changes you, and this one has changed me completely. I put Pony first, every day. I know I've been judged for comparing my business to a baby, but Pony is my baby and he needs me. I also compare my dogs to toddlers on the regular. I'm that person.

Pony Friday is not about being "good enough" to meet current needs. There is no specific customer base we want to steal or tap into; instead we're building something future customers will want to be part of. A brand designed to push people to go after what they love. My goal wasn't to work for myself simply to have ownership of my time and my career. I describe Pony Friday as a motivational lifestyle brand, but it's still a new concept. We're still defining who we are. We're growing into it like an awkward teenager. We're about chasing down dreams like they're already ours. Pony Friday is about growing dreams; it's not about marketing, branding, public speaking or selling products—so our path forward is different. You'll never find our things for sale in stores. You'll never be able to get our stuff anywhere except directly from us. That's how we want it. We want you to have a Pony Friday experience and the added benefit of being showered with enthusiasm about chasing your dreams.

Try Meandering Off the Deep End

It might seem to you like I'm living in a fantasy world, but Pony Friday is real to me. Think of this act of writing as me jumping off a fifty-foot cliff into a pool of excitement below. It's a total rush of anxiety. I've chased Pony too far down the rabbit hole to ever come back. Frankly, I prefer it this way—living a less predictable life that requires my brain to be on all the time. In the Pony Friday world, I get to be exactly who I want to be. I needed to be part of something bigger than my surroundings and myself. I needed something to believe in. Something spellbinding. And Pony Friday is enchanting. You can't say our name with a frown on your face. It's a coupling of two of the happiest words in the world. I'm only off my rocker a little.

Pony Friday is a living, breathing monstrosity. I'd do next to anything for Pony; he's my own flesh-ish and blood-ish. Striding out on your own to start a business isn't a small thing. Most people will think about doing it at some point during their lifetime and a few will be courageous enough to actually do it. Most will shrink back to the comforts of a steady paycheque and working for others. A certain amount of control and autonomy is appealing, but too much and suddenly we experience the burden of having to lead and motivate ourselves. You have to expect the best. The world wants you to work hourly for someone else and it's hard to get work on your own—and even tougher to get the exposure you need to grow. Don't play small.

That doesn't mean you won't start small or take small steps. Just don't play the game small. Don't think small.

Welcome to My Office

When I started Pony Friday, I worked at kitchen tables—mine mostly, but also wherever I went: my sister's condo, my grandma's sewing room (technically not a kitchen table), my parents' house and wherever my latest creative partner lived. My kitchen was a great first office. Most good things start in the kitchen. I've read about other start-ups getting going in garages, but I'm a fan of being close to food. I'm not a chef, but being able to cook while brainstorming has its advantages. It also means forgetting about things on the stove and overcooking them. Pots have boiled over. It's not the safest habit in the world.

You could view the absence of dedicated office space as a lack of commitment to running my own company, or think that I'm cheap and didn't want to spend any money on furniture. Both are true. I wasn't even trying to work remotely—I was just trying to avoid being tied down. I recall one time during my second year in business, when I had all of my latest ideas and notes covering the wall and hutch next to my table. There were stickies about client projects, personal thoughts, money I owed, and invoices coming in. I felt so empowered and organized with this setup—until people came over to eat. Close your eyes and picture yourself hosting a meal with people sitting around your desk. One side of the table sat staring at my business secrets, and as you might imagine it was an uncomfortable feeling. I was smarter the next time and covered the wall and hutch with several large sheets of paper, but that was the moment it was apparent to all that I needed a dedicated office.

I hunted high and low for a desk that would suit my coastal cottage taste and ordered a chair to match. Their price tags were also a great reminder of why I shouldn't deviate from my usual habit of purchasing spendier items gently used, but I splurged.

Shut Up, I'm Thinking

I need the power of silence to create. Nine-to-five boundaries were never my thing. I always ended up working in the evenings and on weekends to harness the moments when I felt most inspired. Nine-to-five was born so that managers could oversee production and I've never enjoyed working with people watching me. Yuck! Collaboration has its place, but I prefer to get lost in the process and not be reminded of the existence of other humans. You actually have the ability to gather everything you need; all you have to do is commit and make your exit.

Now I was in business for the long haul. I had a beautiful desk and a nice chair and a space in the house zoned for Pony Friday. This area started out as a chunk of my living room and was upgraded to its own converted bedroom office space at the end of year three. Some might think the idea of having a roaming office for three years is unpleasant, but while I was going through these growing pains I had no idea it would take that long for me to carve out a dedicated space. Having an adaptable mindset and a roaming office felt contemporary; it was my version of business normal.

Follow the Trickle of Clues

Back in my pre-Pony agency days, I switched from art direction to copywriting—and there were clues leading me to that move, clues that I ignored at first. In ad school, I would often pitch in words here and there—and I was good at it. At the agency, we were always short on writers, so I wrote where and when it was needed to get the job done. People kept suggesting I write, but I would dismiss the idea. Just because you noticed a hole and you're able to fill it doesn't mean that you should. Other people will always pressure "someone else" to pick up the slack on the things that need to get done. So, pay attention and consider pursuing it—but only if you have a knack for it and you enjoy it and it keeps showing up. I didn't choose copywriting. It chose me. And as soon as its talons gripped my fingers, art direction felt like I was dating the wrong person. We had to break up and it wasn't easy. Breakups never are.

I'm constantly shifting. Job security is a myth. Heck, life security is a myth. I aspire to get all of the information possible before I make a decision, but it ultimately has to feel right. And since I'm against wasting time, especially my own, I gather all the information I can as quickly as possible and make a decision. I often go against what the research and so-called sound minds are telling me. I believe it's necessary when you're creating something new. You can't shift out of today's reality if you aren't willing to step off the well-trodden path. Follow the clues; the evidence for taking the path that's right for you might become clear.

- Listen to what you say to others.
- Honour your inner voice.
- Clear your mind of negative thoughts.
- Ask yourself what you want.
- Try new things and visit new places.
- Talk to people who are doing things that interest you.
- Hone your intuition to what feels right to you.

Somewhere deep down there's a part of you that knows what you should be doing. Too bad the whole world seems to have been designed to convince you otherwise. The task is to help that part of you that knows to speak up. Sometimes my inner voice whispers to me in indiscernible mumbles; other times its hollers are deafening. If you listen hard enough, you'll hear your own voice telling you what decisions to make to fit the world around you. There will be times you need to bend, and times you need to hold strong, be patient and allow the world to bend to you. When your friends hold you back with "you're not like that" statements, they're making excuses for why you shouldn't act the way you're acting. Excuses are tricky. Other people will try to put you in a box. You don't belong in one box; you're a compilation of many boxes, dozens, hundreds, maybe even thousands.

THERE'S NO WINNING IF YOU REFUSE TO PLAY

Your Perspective Is Everything

I subscribe to an understanding that life is not entirely random and meaningless. I find the alternative—that human existence is irrelevant and everything I encounter has zero significance—to be depressing. Who wants to live that way? Not me. If our lives are in fact self-directed adventures, we have choice after choice. And with choice comes power. And with power comes a life worth living. My trick is to see my entire life as an elaborate game that takes anywhere from eighty to a hundred years to play—I plan on living a long time. And if life is a game, you don't have to take it so seriously. You can approach moments that are heartrendingly difficult with more ease: *That turn wasn't fun, but look, it's almost my turn to roll the dice again—and things are bound to go better this round.* How about money? Sometimes I

Step Aside for the Dream Train

Imagine your life is a train going quickly down the tracks. Other trains whoosh by you without much sound, and can be dangerous if you get in their way or derail them. Life can get pretty messy when we resist the direction our train is moving in. If your train is chugging along at a steady speed toward your goals and you put the brakes on because you're scared or you're not ready or you're resisting where life is taking you, it's going to create a whole lot of noise. Smooth sailing requires embracing forward motion and all the discomfort that comes with it, which some-times means yelling at those around you to get out of the way.

have it, sometimes I don't. We won't benefit from every turn and that's life. If you stop playing on a bad turn, if you cross your arms and stomp off pouting, things will go sideways. There's no way to win if you refuse to play. Let that sink in. *You have to play.*

My inner voice yells, *Dreams don't have rules.* I can ride a debt wave and push the boundaries of the world as I know it, refusing to accept less than what I can imagine. I have to believe it's going to happen. You have to believe it too. Mondays can feel like Fridays. Your life can be a perpetual Saturday-like existence, but getting there

Stick to Your Plan

Most people I meet have a tough time saying no to social obligations. Many of us suffer from a fear of missing out, and FOMO is debilitating. It also makes it challenging to say yes when you're wondering if something better will come along. I'm completely committed to my path and I know I'll need to sacrifice things to pursue my dreams. That's a price I'm willing to pay. Getting one step closer to my dream, or being there when someone blows out their birthday candles? It's become an easy decision for me. Perspective can be powerful. I want you to live your life on your own terms, not on social pressures, guilt or FOMO. You should have a deep fear of missing out on your own dreams. There should be no greater fear than that.

is going to be uncomfortable. Living outside society's norm isn't easy. Discomfort is the price of entry and every day will have its own learning curve. One million to one is better odds than zero.

Participating is all most humans do in life: they get their participation ribbon and that's enough for them. I play to win, not just to participate. As an entrepreneur, trying is the road to winning. When you win on your own terms, personal satisfaction is your crown.

You Need a Push to Dream Bigger

In year two of Pony Friday, I was writing copy for an executive leadership company and churning out some in-your-face headlines to attract new members to their organization. I seemed to be channelling the words from somewhere else as I typed them onto the page. This was some bold, goading copy, and I was pumped to take it to my client for review. My clients know my evolving business model, and on that day one of them asked me, "Do you ever read your own copy?" For a moment I squirmed in uncomfortable silence. I was proud of the work I was presenting and had interpreted this comment in a negative way. Obviously, I read my own copy, and this batch was great stuff—some of my best. So, what was her deal? And. Then. It. Struck. Me. While these headlines were perfect for this leadership organization, they were also fitting words for me, a growing entrepreneur. All of my pressure to succeed comes from deep within my core, but it's the external push that helps me go the extra mile.

- Kick it up a thousand notches.
- You're at the top of a molehill.
- Stretch beyond your limits.
- Prepare to be pushed.
- Give your life a promotion.
- Tossing in the towel is for quitters.

We're socially conditioned to choose between the things we want. Family or career. Romance or stability. Happy marriage or happy children. The dog or the guy. Being nice or being successful. You're somehow deemed a fool if you think you can have both. And I used to buy that. I used to think there were limits on the things I could have and achieve. Not anymore. I've decided that I can be an anomaly. I'm forty-one. Never been married. No kids. And I've only ever had a creative career. It's true, I've held a sufficient number of yes-I-will-do-this-to-fill-the-gap jobs. You name it: I've played hostess and waitress, dog sitter, babysitter, gravel shoveller, firewood stacker, house cleaner and semi-truck-cab cleaner, folder of random people's laundry, tosser of freshly cut logs from cutlines way out in the bush, grocery packer, shelf stocker and liquor bottle duster. I've retrieved grocery carts from the far reaches of parking lots with their wheels jammed up with snow, and I've even mucked a few stalls—which means that I've literally shovelled shit for pay. Shitty pay. When terrible jobs are temporary, they can actually be kinda fun, and I believe that my dream is worth every roll-up-my-sleeves moment.

You Be You, but the Fun You

In this atmosphere thick with adulting you've probably forgotten how to play. How long can you suppress your inner child before you birth a midlife crisis? I'm like a kid clearing the table so I can go outside and play. I never lose sight of my goals. When is the last time you honoured your own needs? Finding your inner child could be the key to figuring out how to behave boldly. What would your six-year-old self do? How long ago did you abandon yourself in order to be responsible or to fit in? Do you even remember how fun you used to be? Back then if you hated the taste of beans, you'd wrinkle your nose and make a fuss. Stop hiding your feelings and your opinions. You've made decisions before. You prefer oranges over apples. Stop saying "oh, it doesn't matter" when you want to go for sushi over burgers. It *does* matter. If you honour those small feelings and decisions, it makes it easier to honour the big ones. You say it doesn't matter because you haven't been validated. Sure, society places limits on us, but we also put limits on ourselves. Those limitations are hard to see.

I knew a man who worshipped stock car racing but never went to a race. He would watch it on television, but he desperately wanted to go to one of the big races in person and sit among the sea of other fans. He wanted to feel the adrenaline of the live crowd and hear the engines up close. He had put roadblocks in his mind: it was too expensive, tickets were impossible to get. Yet, crowds of millions attend these races every year. I sassily told him to "just go" and his response was, "It's not that easy!" What? Stop the car! It's as easy as you decide it is, buddy. The thing about small wins is that they set you up for even bigger wins. You build your way up with a can-do attitude. When you're committed to finding a path to get there, your thoughts get focused on solutions. That's all you need to do. Just get your superhuman brain-machine stalking solutions. Building your world and being in the zone means adopting a childlike curiosity. You cannot afford to be afraid to express the things you like.

You don't have to get me or like me. Maybe you're into eating jujubes on pizza. Good for you. Want to roller skate in your pajamas at two in the morning? Go for it. That doesn't hurt anyone. Somewhere along the way maybe you forgot about yourself and what you actually like. Own your weirdness and march on. I like to sing voice messages for my friends and a cappella my daily activities.

When I sit down with a friend and bring my enthusiasm, I plant seeds of possibility. I didn't know I would someday be in front of audiences at conferences, planting those seeds in the minds of attendees. Tiny, consistent steps keep your dreams growing! You might not be able to see the whole thing yet, so focus on one part. The gut-tingling reason you want to go to that local coffee shop today could be a step for you, the one that gets to the next step, and the next, as you build your dream-chaser toolbox. You might have an experience

MONDAYS CAN FEEL LIKE FRIDAYS

that guides you to do something. Not doing that one little thing you feel compelled to do might end up rotting away the part of you that wants to shoot for the stars or go to the moon. Give yourself permission to honour the dream inside of you. Other people say no to me all the time. It's my job to say yes to myself and to chase my dreams with vigour. You have to believe that you can achieve mythical proportions—after all, you taught yourself to walk and that's huge.

Stop Kidding Yourself

A lady I know told me about this idea she and her husband had that would change the lives of a lot of people. I'm telling you, this idea is so needed. And they're working hard on it, she said—one day a month. I burst out laughing, right in her face. I hadn't meant to be rude, but twelve days a year sounded absurd to me. That isn't enough. One day per month is hardly an improvement over zero days per month. Let's imagine that they put in eight hours a day each of those twelve days—that's less than a hundred hours per person, and zero momentum. Pay close attention to the things that swindle your focus away from your dreams.

Stretch Your Dreams Even Bigger

Getting out of your comfort zone is imperative. That's where the rewards are. Even if the only reward is proving to yourself that you'll be fine. What I find most interesting about leaving my comfort zone is that I evolve and grow to occupy a new one. I can never go back to the old zone. The old zone becomes uncomfortable. It's now too constricting for me. And it's tough to look back and imagine that I was ever that stuck.

Behaving Boldly Used to Be Your Thing

As an infant, you were bold and direct without even a second thought. You cried whenever you were hungry, thirsty, bored or wanted attention. That might be instinct working in your favour, or perhaps it's survival of the loudest. Imagine now that you dared to shout out your unfiltered needs, shelved your excessive consideration for those around you, demanded what you wanted right now and fussed until you got it. Being bold and direct will get you things a lot faster than being bashful, subtle or manipulative. No, I'm not suggesting that you go around crying, but being clear about what you need is essential to getting it. How else would anyone know?

The Pony Goes in Front of the Cart

If you believe in your dreams, you will make time for them. Make your dreams one of your top priorities and see how your life shifts around them. If you've ever had a baby or adopted a puppy, you'll get this concept. Suddenly, there is no option other than to tend to this new little creature's needs. Move your dreams up the list until they start bumping other less important things out of the way.

I work on Pony Friday stuff before I work on client stuff. It's how I'm growing my business. It's the only way I can move anything forward. I don't want to be the proverbial shoemaker that walks around barefoot. From time to time, I've helped advertising agencies with their own brand evolution, because they have been forever busy working on things for their clients. And I have to tell you, they drag this process out for months and months, and sometimes never come back to it. That's shoddy reputation management for people known for building reputations. And don't worry about me not getting client work done. I deliver on time because I'll stay up all night to meet a deadline. There's a gap, though, where it's harder to do that for our own stuff and instead, it's tempting to go to bed and finish it tomorrow.

This procrastinator behaviour—stealthily wrapped in self-care—is why I tackle my Pony Friday stuff first, because "tomorrow" never comes!

For example, in year five, I took a contract with a big Toronto advertising agency and made oodles of cash, which would have been wonderful if it weren't for the fact that my contribution to Pony Friday fizzled down to nothing. I was so burned out from being at my client's beck and call for ten weeks straight that I wasn't living much of a life. There's always a split between having time and having money. I had to take a good hard look at myself and ask what kind of life I wanted to live and what was more important: making a lot of money, because I'd clearly found some solid ways to earn it—or living a better existence and making a meaningful contribution.

> NEVER BACK DOWN BECAUSE IT'S TOO HARD

I no longer take contracts with companies that treat people as their personal workhorses. This choice is not without consequences, but I embrace the messiness the best I can, and I've even started laughing at the state of my finances. What a wild ride this has been so far. Sometimes money seems slippery, and other times it seems slimy. We'll talk more about the m-o-n-e-y later. Things work out for me. Not always in the way I planned, but it's good in the end. I have what I need. And I force myself to continue to believe this even when it seems the furthest thing from the truth.

Learn from the Rut

I like big ruts. They remind me that it's time to shuffle things around. My entire life is a slippery slope into a comfortable rut and I'm willing to bet yours is too. Our friends enjoy the predictability of our interactions; that's how trust is built. Relationships depend on stability,

Count Your Opinion First

Remind yourself to let go of outside opinions—don't let the world brainwash you into forgetting your dreams. Sometimes awareness comes in the form of unease or stress, and it knots up in my stomach when I'm playing too small. I need to rise higher and take ownership of my authentic path. Censor your shoulds and stop worrying about what the world will think.

which is built on routines. When I'm resistant to change, my daily habits become more ingrained and permanent. If negative things become habits, we're in trouble, since "easier" today often means more long-term pain, while "difficult" today usually means things will eventually get easier. I know that in order to *do* better I have to *be* better. There are good routines worth keeping and old routines that are no longer serving you. Here are some signs you're in a rut:

- You complain about the same things all the time.
- You're always living for the weekend.
- Your life has started to bore you.
- You're not mentally stimulated by anything.
- You can't remember what you're working for.
- You're replaying your last vacation in your head.
- You can't stop focusing on what's missing.

That Friday Feeling

You can expand your happy as wide as you want, or you can have a case of the Mondays every day of the week. It's up to you. I broke free from the concept of Monday to Friday. Make your own Pony Friday and don't hold back until you have that Friday feeling more often than you don't.

You might feel stressed at the thought of going financially all in. And that used to be me, afraid to stick my little piggy-bank neck out. But after one good look at the predictable and boring horizon in front of me, I changed the direction of my life. If I'd kept my full-time gig, I'd be sitting pretty, mortgage free with a heap of retirement savings. Yep, sitting pretty in a boring-ass room with beige walls ready to retire from Dullsville. Now, instead of that bleak existence, I'm real estate free and neck-deep in debt. My brain might be wired differently from yours—entrepreneurs raised me, so I was breastfed on stress. My parents started out with nothing. The vehicle I drive is worth as much as their first house. Maybe that's more of an argument about inflation, but I think you catch my drift. Even if you don't, it's not as though I'm near enough for you to glare at.

Have the Guts to Go with Your Gut

What's your path of truth? Where could that truth lead you? Do you have the guts to go for it? Maybe you have no idea what trusting your gut means. If you're thinking of a growl from your stomach that demands pizza, you're not far off. You know what food you like and what food you don't like. You have a favourite kind of music, vacation spot and stores you like to go to. You know who to trust and who not to. Every time you honour your own preferences, you hone your instincts. If my friend invites me to a party and for some reason I don't want to go, I own it and stay home. They might get a polite no, or a "why the fuck would I want to do that?" My gut told me not to go. It doesn't have to be any more complicated than that. The difficulty comes when the decisions have more resting on the line and the answers are seemingly less clear. Some of the stuff that I want requires me to do things that aren't so fun. Say, attending a wedding for someone I want to keep in my life for the next forty years. And having a horse means shovelling manure—for free. Sacrifices must be made.

FORCE YOUR LIFE TO SHIFT AROUND YOUR DREAMS

I never back down from things I've started when they get too hard, and sometimes I have to trick myself into doing things that need to get done when I don't feel inclined. My existence is as human as yours—it's not always the funnest, but disappointing yourself is optional. When I'm paralyzed and suffering from inaction, my entire body might as well be buried in sand, with only my face sticking out. Quitting is always an option. Every step you take away from your dreams is kicking a little bit of dirt on the coffin where your best self sleeps. Rest in peace, big dreams. Rest in peace.

Let's say you're in desperate need of money and there's a job on the table. It pays well, but you'd have to work with an incredibly difficult client and the experience would make your entire life miserable for a month. Maybe you need to suck it up and stop being a baby; after all, you do need the money. On the other hand, what if you trusted that your opportunities were supposed to be positive and challenging, so you pass up this job with the belief that there will be a better one right around the corner, with a more desirable client. That's what I call trust. You know instinctively that something superior is coming, so you don't feel pressured to take a gig that isn't right for you. The next level up is staying relaxed and believing that it's on its way and that it will arrive before your credit card bill is due.

I think some of this has to do with faith. I'm not religious. I'd classify myself as spiritual and a pony-sized believer in universal energy. What you believe in doesn't make much difference when you're in

Take This Plan and Shove It

Five-year plans are for predictable paths. The world moves quickly. With new information coming in constantly, it's hard to believe crafting a long-term plan is worth your time. I love long-term dreams and pursuing them with vigour, but you have to adjust your sails and be ready for the storms to redirect you to uncharted seas. Uncharted seas that might lead you discover new lands. New lands with the riches you've been searching for. A beach with a treasure chest filled with your dreams.

agreement that there's something out there helping to connect the dots. When I trust my intuition and do the work available to do, I can relax knowing that what's meant to be is on its way.

I said that I *can* relax, I did not say that I *do* relax—but I try.

Turn Your Can'ts into Canters

Who do you want to be when you grow up? Go all in on that. I promise that you're not too old to pursue it. You can refurbish your life anytime you want to. One day, a thousand sleeps from now, you might wake up and realize that you could have done it sooner. It took me six years before I truly got in the game. So what if you feel stuck in the unknown and can't figure out what your dream is? You may have buried it so deep you think it's long gone and you can't get it back. Start digging. Change can happen now. It can be slow or abrupt.

When I was little, I wanted to be this famous nature artist I'd seen in mall galleries, crossed with a soccer player. Once I understood life a bit better, I realized that becoming someone else was impossible. That particular artist was also a man—and an old one. Although I'm still struck by his paintings, I know that being myself is considerably more rewarding than magically becoming an old-man-soccer-player-painter. I continue to pursue a creative career with a side of sports—creativity first, above all else. What did you want to do when you were a kid? Does any of that still resonate? It can be fun to resurrect past interests and see if they still light you up. I highly recommend forgetting your "potential" and getting right into action. I am capable of many things, but knowing my capacity and applying those abilities are miles apart. It starts with conviction. If you're a high achiever who's settling for less than you should have or could have, it's time to chase your dreams with tenacity.

CHASE YOUR DREAMS WITH TENACITY

I Know What I'm Doing

Nah, I don't know what I'm doing. None of us know what we're doing all the time. Marinate in that. It's a doozy. You could be reading this thinking I have a pretty good handle on things. But many times I don't.

Saying "I don't know what I'm doing" might be the most catastrophic thing that any of us ever tell ourselves. It makes us feel frail and incompetent, which we aren't. There are varying measures of confidence, and you simply need to grow yours. I've been growing mine my entire life, but sometimes jerks come along and hack large branches off my self-esteem tree to burn in their own ego-building bonfires. Combatting that takes a whole lot of positive self-talk and a reminder that world-class gardeners prune trees to help them flower more and produce more fruit. Let's self-talk our way to the top with some basic assumptions:

- I know where I'm going.
- I know what I'm doing.
- I won't ever stop going and doing.
- I was born to keep trying.
- I've got this.
- Seriously, whatever this is—I've got it.

These are the right kind of affirmations, since clearly you and I do know something about what we're doing. I know what I'm doing, even when I'm scared of the responsibilities that come with that type of statement. I'm forever growing into the person and leader that Pony Friday needs. I'm not there yet and I'll always be playing catch-up, like a new parent unsure of what their child needs.

Satisfaction Is Your Nemesis

When you start out, you'll be naïvely optimistic. You have to be. I thought, *How hard could being an entrepreneur be?* The simple fact that chasing your dreams isn't easy makes going after them extra special. You'll want to quit. Does everyone go through this amount of struggle? Yes, I believe they do. Few are daring enough to do it, so don't quit until you get what you want.

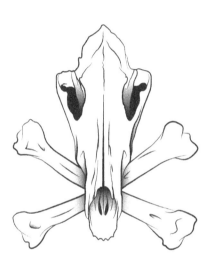

2

IGNORE
THE
HERD

Let Me Get My Frog

Flashback alert! I'm taking you way back to 1983. It was Thanksgiving and I was about to turn five. My entire family had gathered for supper at my parents' place. It was a fabulous celebration with aunts, uncles and cousins.

I was in my element and wasn't afraid of being my full self. These people truly knew me, and I was a child and did what I pleased. When it came time to take a family photo, I ran to my room to grab this amazing froggy party hat that I'd recently gotten at a friend's birthday. It was complete with big eyes, a classic pink cartoon mouth and long green legs that hung down on either side of my face. Naturally, I thought this was the perfect occasion for froggy to shine. I was super pumped... but the rest of my family was not, especially my parents. Apparently, his shamrock skin tone didn't go with the beautiful autumnal colour palette.

They didn't understand how important it was for him to be in the picture. A frog on my head would obviously make this a better photo.

We negotiated—them trying to convince me to remove the hat, and me trying to get them to see reason. Well, negotiations failed and the situation quickly escalated into a fashion-police chase. I remember little paper frog legs flapping in the wind as I ran around the yard with them after me.

Look through our photo album, and you won't find a boring cookie-cutter family. You'll find a family with a little kid who's never looked happier—with a green frog atop her head.

When you look back on your life, were you brave enough to stand out? Were you bold enough to do what you wanted? Did you fight against all odds? I mean, I had, like, twenty family members who were all bigger than me, besides my baby sister, and none of them could stop me. And, in fact, in the photo, my sister is staring at me, clearly thinking, *I wanna be like her.*

Former Perfectionists Rejoice

I haven't *always* been as self-assured as I was in that moment when I fought for froggy's right to be in our family photo. In high school, I had a crippling relationship with perfection. In art class, I was teacher's pet. In every other class, I got scraping-for-a-pass marks, but in art I would get one hundred percent almost every time. I strove for perfection, and when I didn't land top marks I would be so furious that I'd crumple up my latest masterpiece and throw it in the trash, right in front of my teacher and classmates. Talk about crazy—tossing out a beautiful piece of work because an art teacher said it wasn't a ten out of ten. My vanity could not accept anything less than perfection; validated creativity was my definition of self. Obviously, that's sad and problematic—needing that level of approval. Yikes. Had I not let go of perfection, I'd likely have died of an anxiety attack or become a dull human stuck in the attempt to achieve it. I've now taken that child who needed external validation and turned her into a woman who knows what's good and what isn't, and rates her own creations on her own scale. It's insane to me now that I would give a speck of consideration to what some narrow-minded high school art teacher thought of me—or my work. I took fine arts in university, and fully embodied the student who teachers didn't connect with, and I suffered from lower grades because of it.

Ranking your own opinion above all others isn't exactly firm footing when you start—unless you're a narcissist, but I'll assume you aren't. Going with your own gut often takes practice. I assume it will be a lifelong effort for me, equivalent to working out my body to stay fit. And these days fitness is hit and miss—but it's the thought that counts. No, it's really not. I need to stay in control of my thoughts. Your inner voice may start out shaky and unsure. We're conditioned to look outside ourselves. We're trained to seek the opinions of those in authority positions for validation that we are good, have done well, and are worthy of praise.

PERFECTION IS A PRISON

Resilient people tend to find that validation inside their own hearts. They acknowledge the opinions of others as perspectives, not facts. We all have unique life experiences and past moments we deemed profound or jarring. It's our job as adults to evaluate our reference points for what warrants our attention and what does not. We decide what gets classified as historic and worth keeping, and what gets tossed out.

Killing off my insecurities was the best thing I ever did. I haven't gotten them all yet; I swear they continue to swarm in like wasps at a barbeque. There will always be more to annihilate. Do you remember the last time you killed off or let go of a piece of your old self? You need to keep zapping those pesky buzzing invaders, and pruning back fruit trees so they produce more. You won't truly know what you're capable of until you let go of what's holding you back.

It's not perfect. I'm not perfect. Nothing I do is perfect. I repeat. I'm not perfect. Thinking that you can't possibly show anyone your masterpiece until you make it perfect is creative hell. I've forced myself to say goodbye to this way of thinking. I had to. Perfection is a prison. Identifying as a perfectionist cripples any chance we have at progress.

Yes, I get scared to share my creations. With my limited budgets and resources, I can often see that my best is not The Best. It's only *my* best and the best my team could do right now with the time and resources we had. I say goodbye to the perfectionist's way of thinking on a daily basis. It's constantly showing up at my door petitioning for my subscription, and I refuse to pay the fee.

Sometimes I post something, then want to barf and hide. Maybe eat a bag of chips and crawl into bed with the covers pulled over my head—a luxury available to you when you work from home. Worse is when I post something a bit edgy and feel insecure about it, then someone asks, "Why did you post that?" I don't have the kind of resolve that allows me to feel okay with such questions. My answer? "I need to post weird things now to prepare my mind to post even weirder things later." I do my best with what I have and keep moving. Most things are fixable. And if I can't fix it, I can usually grow from it. By all means, be intentional. Be swift. But under no circumstances am I suggesting that you intentionally slap things together. Never. Ever. Do. That. Simply do your best with what you have and what you know, get it done and then move on.

Make Friends with Fear

The scariest things have the most potential to help you grow. I was pretty freaked out before my first talk. I'm great with anyone one-on-one, but centre stage felt overwhelming. I had physical jitters and was on an adrenaline rush. The entire thing went a bit sideways, but it was real...maybe a bit too real. I'll never have my first talk again—that ship has sailed, and with it a cargo load of heebie-jeebies. Now I know to shake off my discomfort with some high kicks, and commit to accepting my best as whatever it turns out to be. You have to be able to take hit after hit; you're a rock in a tumbler getting your rough edges worn off. You have to go all in!

Obviously, we're adults, and we get overwhelmed, stressed, anxious, nervous, concerned and worried. All of that boils down to fear. Admit it, you hesitate. Or worse. You freeze. I get scared all the time. Do as much research as you can to set yourself up for success, but don't avoid doing the thing you're scared of because you don't know everything you need to know. You will never know everything you need to know.

> **CLAIM YOUR PLANET**

Sometimes, the more you know, the less you feel you know. You have to get comfortable moving ahead with less information. Make a decision. Move forward. Then continue to make decisions and move with them. Pleasing everyone is impossible. Don't try. Even completely pleasing *myself* can sometimes feel out of reach. Write your options out on paper, do a pros and cons list if you need to, and choose one. Just pick the best thing for now. Stay tuned for my mom's notepaper strategy. If you need to, you can think of your choices as for-now decisions until you can improve on them later. Be positive and know that the future will present ample opportunities to course correct.

Planet Elise Has Its Own Solar System

Fitting in is something we all struggle with at different points in our lives. We keep searching for a place to fit, and forget that we could build one. Yes, you *can* create a place where you feel good. It might be a sanctuary in your home, a garden in your yard, a camping spot in the woods, the summit of a ski hill, a recreational sports team or a corporate culture. Being friends with everyone is a terrible strategy and it's pretty much impossible, so look for synergies. Chances are, there are others kinda like you who are also dissatisfied with the standard interpretation of life and want to unsubscribe. It's powerful to spend time with someone who's being one hundred percent themselves. Planet Elise is a creatively nerdy place and I love it, because I built it that way and it's mine. Claim *your* planet.

The world tricks us into believing that creativity and "arts" cannot support us, or that it can only support a fortunate few. It's never presented as a viable option to choose for a career. I have a theory on why the world tries to keep us from the unknown of creativity. I think the universe needs to know we want it bad enough to fight for it. I'm willing. Are you?

Forego Fitting In

I highly recommend giving serious thought to the people who you spend time with: they're the ones influencing you. Let's flashback to college me. I started my post-secondary education studying fine arts. As a creative misfit, that seemed the only logical place to go, and I wasn't that popular with my non-artsy high school friends. Unless you think about how much they liked to make fun of me. While everyone else was studying science, education or something more "practical" like business, I was in art and my projects were optimal for teasing.

While on break from university, a group of my friends were hanging out in my parents' basement. I'd been showing them some of my projects when the person I was dating took a rope sculpture I'd made from found objects and hung it around their neck. To my horror, they proceeded to dance around like a baboon. (No offence to baboons here; in truth, I have no idea how they dance.) I felt so emotionally body-slammed and disrespected. Everyone laughed. It was humiliating. What an inconsiderate bunch of turd munchers. For this and many other reasons, I no longer consider any of those nitwits my friends. If your friends don't support you, dump them.

I regularly edit my "herd" to ensure it has the best dynamic for my present and future. The past is done. Now could be a good time for you to exit the herd. To be honest, the goodbyes can be awkward. If you exit Elise style, it's gonna be a full-on breakup. Fade-aways are only good for leaving house parties—they aren't ideal for ending best-friends-forever relationships. There is a wake of former friends behind me. Living my own definition of life meant letting go of previous notions others had about me. I had to shut off any caring about what they thought. This is my journey. I am constantly cutting my heart off from what others think of me. It's a peculiar thing that seems to grow back. I know I'll never be completely rid of it, which is annoying. Keep in mind that ghosting just leaves things unsaid, and make no mistake, that stuff will haunt you.

EYE-POPPING STRESS AND BUCKETS OF FUN

Forget what others say. I had to stop airing my frustrations to non-entrepreneurs because they would just tell me to go get a job, which sounds to me like applying to go to prison. The fact that they didn't get it cracked open a crevasse between us that couldn't be crossed. Choosing a lesser-known path is too uncomfortable for most citizens to deal with—and it's not the change that's scary, it's the aftermath. Change triggers a domino effect and there is no going back. It's like tossing a rock into a canyon: look out below.

Anchoring to your old life is useless in creating your new one. You can invite people on your path and you can share where you're headed, but you can't drag them with you. Lead by example. You doing your own thing will give others the idea that it's okay to do their own thing too. Just don't expect it of them. You can't know the fear they struggle with or the reasoning behind their decisions.

The Ambitious One

I'm an ambitious person. I can own that. I was even once introduced to a group of women at a party as "the ambitious one" and that felt accurate. I'm not sure if that introduction was done snootily or not, but it's true. And I can own the facts. I'm ambitious. And I hope I've only seen the tip of my ambition iceberg, because this is still the beginning to me. You can want big things, dream about them and talk about them all you like, but if you don't work for your goals they're as good as dead. It's like wanting a fire and refusing to rub two sticks together or even simply to strike the match.

My past is always pulling me back into the folds of its fat. It keeps calling (literally—people will call and try to convince me to work for them) and I will have to remind them and myself that I am now on a different path, searching for a more meaningful contribution. My expectations of going out on my own were lofty, yet even a couple of years in, not much in my day-to-day had changed. I owned my job. I wanted to build something that I could be part of for a long time without an agency-client relationship. I was questioning everything. I still am because I know this can't be *it* for me. What should I be working on? Where should I be working? Who should I be working with? I didn't want to wait until I was in my sixties to start thinking about my legacy. I might die before then.

Five years was a milestone. It's the middle marker between zero and ten, which means I'm now on the other side of the rapidly closing gap between start-up land and being a well-established entity. Make no mistake, we're still wayfinding. It takes a long time for the world to take you seriously. You might spend four years at university, for example, just to get an education that leaves you with nothing more than a piece of paper. All you'll have to your name is a pile of debt. Your first few years into your career are about finding your footing. And that's where we're at with Pony Friday: a lot of lessons and a pile of debt. We have our get-this-business-off-the-ground degree, and now we're figuring out the next part. You know, the whole make a difference in the world and some serious cha-ching in your bank account.

The next few years will be filled with surprises and we will definitely outdo past achievements. Insane work, personal growth, eye-popping stress and buckets of fun—yes, fun! Just like when socks were once the biggest mountain we'd climbed.

My Sock Mountain Isn't Laundry

How did I end up with a rental unit full of Pony Friday socks? Well, have you ever wanted things that nobody else had? Oh yes, this item is exclusive from my closet and you can't have it—too bad for you. I like the idea of wearing my own things, but there are some solid reasons why I should not have stepped into clothing retail. No retail experience. The closest I've come is working at a grocery and liquor store—but let's be honest, those two sell themselves. Zero merchandise experience with no connections to manufacturers—where do you even get this stuff? My fashion sense has never been celebrated. I have yet to set any trends (unless you consider the time my sister and I bought blue-and-white-striped-railroad-conductor-style overalls at the workwear store while waiting for our dad—overalls that all the girls at our high school suddenly wanted). And I lack general trendiness. I wear what I want to—we'll get to my bright collection of Super Boss pants later.

Also, I have no real experience designing clothes, beside a childhood of sewing clothes for my dolls and that one time when I attempted to make myself a dress out of a shower curtain. To be fair, I have been sewing stuff my entire life—occasionally from patterns and many times without. Talent lives in me, and in the right environment it comes out to play. I kill at Halloween costumes and used to sew intricate themed get-ups for my best friend and myself. One time, we were disqualified from a costume contest because our outfits appeared to be rented. It was the best compliment at the worst time; we were impeccably dressed as Egyptian goddesses. The fabric for those costumes was feverishly free-cut and sewn together from an idea in my head that came together as I worked. While in the creative zone I become completely bewitched under an artistic spell. I'd put care into every detail, including hand-beaded headpieces, and we lost to a man wearing a giant foam penis. Clearly, we had the wrong crowd.

None of my experience has anything to do with clothing designs that people might like and wear. And part of me doesn't care if anyone else likes anything we make, because I like it. Forget trends and logic. Let quirkiness reign. I never let logic stop me. We're talking about my dreams. I'm more than willing to defy logic and

YOU WIN SOME AND YOU LOSE MOST

conventional wisdom in favour of taking risks. Our minds invent dreams that become complex mazes for our imaginations to solve. We must boldly reach for them with the certainty that the power of the universe is behind us, conspiring in our favour. Logic has no place in dream-chasing. So, we dreamed of socks.

My first designer thought it was fun and worked on designs for weeks, making plenty of options for us to choose from. Yes, you read that right: I paid them to work on sock designs for *weeks* before we even had anyone lined up to make them. We had no clue that this sort of thing could take months—make that years. Years. Not. Even. Kidding.

You Share a Country, Not Standards

I scoured the web and found a Canadian factory that claimed to make socks. They got back to us, and charged $250 for prototypes. I'm talking about a tangible thing, a first stab at manufacturing. We had completed the designs and put them through our quality control on what we wanted them to look like.

This is probably as good a place as any to remind you that we had no idea what we were up against and, if you hadn't realized it on your own (we hadn't yet), socks are knit—and those stitches are not perfect little pixel squares or dots on your computer screen, they are tiny squashed rectangular vee shapes. Each stitch is wider than it is tall, which means that your design has to be translated into a foreign knitting-machine language. The factory needs to take your design and convert it into a stitchable pattern. So, your beautiful design that you took months to finesse gets morphed into code for a machine with a stitch count. Joy oh joy.

I've always worked with print and digital media; I'd never worked with knitted goods—except that time I commissioned twelve knit penguin stuffies for a project I worked on with the local zoo, but that was different. There are machines with different needle counts. Different yarn blends and different thicknesses. Maybe $250 was reasonable; it seemed spendy for a couple of pairs of socks. I had no experience in this industry so I paid it and sent our designs. We waited eagerly for what seemed like forever for the prototypes to arrive. I was confident that they would be fabulous. It was our first attempt, and I anticipated success. I knew they would be amazing. I was so giddy when they finally arrived.

Have you ever had your heart broken? I mean broken in a way that's unexpected and cruel. My breath stuck in my throat and my heart stopped. Crushed. That's how I felt after ripping open the delivery pack from the sock factory. They were atrocious. Admittedly, I do have high standards, but these weren't even the right size. They were made for giants who had poor eyesight. So, I did what any normal person feeling a boatload of shame would do, and hid them from myself. I shoved them in a drawer and tried to forget all about them. It didn't work. They were impossible to forget. But I didn't want to look at them again until I had a solution.

The fact that they sent these samples as an example of their work was concerning, and although we had further conversations about improving the prototypes, I decided to cut my losses and try somewhere else. It never occurred to me to ask for a refund, since they had fulfilled their end of the bargain by delivering a prototype. What else could $250 get me? A couple of nice pairs of jeans, a flight somewhere, several bags of dog food, five movie nights or multiple tanks of gas. I try not to think about it. That $250 got me a life lesson. You win some and you lose some.

Another Day, Another Spin of the Wheel

In my factory search, I had found several North American companies willing to make my socks and sell them to me at retail prices, leaving me no profit margin. Maybe I'll get back to them once we start paying each other in jelly beans. I finally found a factory that would make socks for a reasonable price, and their prototypes were only $1,000. I say "only" while rolling my eyes and screaming *Are you kidding me?* in my head. What did I know? I still had next to no experience, and my "business coach" was busy getting me to fill out useless spreadsheets about my sales funnel. The lesson on "win some, lose some" is prevalent in entrepreneurship. I fail on the regular, but I do my best to see these failures as lessons and move on. There isn't really any other option.

We waited for months to get prototypes from sock supplier number two. They kept giving us the runaround: they were busy, their  designer had quit, something about a software update and other lame excuses. Finally, after a lot of follow-up, instead of sending the samples I was pestering them for, they sent our deposit back. Are you kidding me? *This is crazy*, I thought.

PICKY ISN'T A BAD THING

Defeated, I crumpled on the soft creamy white sheepskin rug beside my desk. It's where the dogs lie. I wanted to cry. Tears pushed out from behind my eyelids, desperate for their five minutes of fame. This was their moment. Now my heart was double crushed. My efforts fruitless. All my options seem to have vanished. I had nothing, less than nothing. I'd crashed into the wall at the end of happiness road and in that moment on the rug something changed. I'm unclear on whether a piece of my soul died, or if my resilience was knighted.

I realized that I could either cry or take action. I no longer worked for someone else. I worked for myself. I didn't have the luxury of blubbering. What a waste of time. Nobody is going to pay me to sit on the floor and sob. I'm not an actress. If anything was going to work out, it was going to be because I made it happen. Flashback to prehistoric me, when I hid in the printer room at work a time or two and bawled my eyes out. In an open-concept workspace, you have to make an effort to hide your emotional side from coworkers. Look at me now, people. Look at me now.

Right then and there, I stood up, spun my wooden chair around, flipped open my laptop and started hunting down companies that made socks. Should I be calling factories, manufacturers, sock brands or wholesalers? I was pretty clueless. I called and emailed. I sent our designs and asked what types of socks they offered. Could they make the styles we wanted at a reasonable price? Most contacts I spoke with wouldn't even consider it, or wanted too much per pair. I heard no, after no, after no, and I kept searching, emailing and calling. There was no room for no. I needed a yes. I was desperate for a yes. I wasn't going to settle for less. I was fishing. I kept casting out my line to see if I would get anything. I'd given up on hearing the right words and was simply going through the motions. Clearly, this pond was all fished out.

Then, there was a tug on my line. Finally, I got one. I got my yes. Our first official sock guy was a bit of a bully. He was hard on me, yet incredibly helpful: "I want you to succeed, young lady" blended with "You have no idea what you are doing and I find that hysterical." Here's the catch to the sock thing—free prototypes with a minimum order of 1,200 pairs per style. What? That's one hundred dozen pairs. There weren't that many people in my entire high school. And that wasn't the worst of it. Having one style was not going to cut it, so I ordered three different styles. Selfishly, I ordered two in a standard women's size (thinking of how cute my feet would be in Pony Friday socks and how much I would love to wear them) and one for men. That meant I would have 3,600 pairs of socks. That's three hundred dozen. Fantastic! Let's do it. Now... what was I going to do with 3,600 pairs of socks?

The Pony Friday red is a soft red, but it's still red. The prototypes came back looking fuchsia. Eeek! If you've spent time with designers, you can appreciate how precious we creatives are about colour. It needs to be spot-on or at least very close to spot-on, and this was not. The thread was pink. It was not red. The ball of anxiety in my stomach started to tighten. I had such a tough time finding a manufacturer who would take us seriously, and the only issue with these socks were a slight shade problem. I wondered if perhaps I was being too fussy. I wanted to be happy with them and call it a day, but I knew it would eat me up inside, so I pulled out my brave and I pushed back. Our manufacturer is out of Montreal, but this factory was in China and that makes for quite the game of telephone. You have to tell your contact in Quebec, who has to relay that information to someone overseas, who has to tell the team on the factory floor what we need. I was told I was picky—which I am both familiar with and all right with. I'm also happy, because I got what I wanted. Picky isn't a bad thing if you get something you can be proud of, and we did.

In forty months in business, I hadn't needed a single cheque and was now being asked for a cheque to pay the deposit on our sock order. I didn't have company cheques. The only people in my life who take cheques are horse people: the stable, the farrier and the riding instructor. I had personal cheques. I'd offered to send an e-transfer, but they wouldn't accept it. They said I could wire the money or send a cheque. Wiring money isn't the easiest either, especially when your account is in Canadian funds and your supplier has an American bank account. So, I used one of those generic fill-in-your-name-and-address cheques the bank gives you when you set up an account, then sent it east by courier.

We were a new customer, one that didn't have cheques (yet) and had never done merchandise before, so our supplier was likely nervous about getting paid. That might be why they laughed on the phone and said that if we didn't pay, they would flood the market with Pony Friday socks. Flood the market, ha ha ha, with 3,600 pairs of socks, ha ha ha. To me, it wasn't funny: thousands of pairs was an impressive amount from my perspective. But to them, it was nothing. They dealt in such remarkable volumes that we were more of a pet project. I had to put my pride in my back pocket. It stung, but it's better to be an adorable pet than an unloved street dog. I was restarting at the bottom, maybe not the absolute bottom rung, because I had a lot of life behind me, but I was new at this. My career in advertising was helping me generate income to grow a merchandise line, but it didn't give me any experience in making products to sell. We weren't a charity case, and if we provided our supplier with some entertainment then it was a win for everyone. Let's not forget that being small has an upside. You couldn't flood the market. Very few sets of feet would ever wear our socks, and exclusivity is exactly where we wanted to be. Most businesses making and selling products are looking for distribution channels so they can sell higher volumes. Our plan isn't to offer wholesale products. That's not our jam.

The order was in and all that was left to do was wait. Waiting for your product to be made overseas and then sent by boat can test your patience. It's like waiting for your next birthday when you just had one yesterday (only this was about 120 days to wait, not 364—still long when it was our first order). Plus, once our shipment landed, we didn't get to receive it right away. Get this. We live between the port the ship came into on one side of the country and the warehouse our supplier unpacks it in is on the other side. Call me hopeful: I asked if they could possibly drop our stuff off in Calgary as it went by from west to east, instead of us having to wait for it to be shipped past us and shipped back. I had to have it explained to me that my little pallet of socks was tucked into a shipping container somewhere among a bunch of other orders and that container was just going to get offloaded from the ship and onto a train to be taken across Canada to be unloaded. Then I could have the socks shipped to me. Did I have a courier service we wanted to use for the shipment? Um. Nope. I was so impatient that I sent my person with their truck to get it from the shipping yard in Calgary so I didn't have to wait another day for it to be delivered to our house—besides, residential deliveries are extra. They dropped the pallet right in the back of the pickup and finally the socks were mine.

Socks and Wet Blankets

My excitement was sky high when that pallet of boxes was finally within reach. Months of hard work and un-cried tears had brought me to this moment. Until these words carried through the air: "You have a lot of socks to sell." I froze and took this in for a moment, calculating my response. The person who said them meant well enough, I guess. But it shook my reality that anyone would make such a comment in my moment of joy—my highest high. It was a sharp pin to my balloon. All that was required were some woo-hoos and high-fives. After a moment I located my sass and responded with a cheeky, "Nope. That's just a fresh pair of socks every day for the next nine years." The math was flawed and I likely wouldn't make full use of the men's sized socks, but point made. These socks were mine.

> SUCCESS COMES AFTER HUMILIATING FAILURES

As we were loading them into the house, my partner started tossing the boxes down the stairs to the basement. They were boxes of socks—soft goods that would not be harmed by this efficient manner of relocation. My perspective was different. These were precious goods that I'd wrestled to get for over a year, and they were being carelessly thrown, one after the other, down a flight of stairs. When I saw the boxes tumble and bump to the bottom of the stairs into a heap of cardboard cubes, they didn't seem that valuable at all. I had to pull myself together and find the joy in the moment. I'm in the sock-rock-tumbler of life, and I'll come out with more experience, more confidence, more stories, more compassion and fewer rough edges. At least, that's what I keep telling myself. Staying optimistic is a superpower.

We started designing socks near the end of year three and finally had them in hand at the beginning of year five. It took us eighteen months, like a slow-learning baby taking its first step. No big deal.

This type of process is my normal. Now I'm shifting my energy to sock mountain number two, getting our socks direct from the factory instead of using a middleman. The blisters from that climb have healed, and I'm ready for the next iteration of my odyssey.

Sucking Is Part of the Process

How long can you endure the suck? Sometimes I struggle with feeling as though I'm not getting anywhere. Month after month of chipping away at giant goals can leave you feeling like nothing is happening. It is. The shifts are still just too tiny to see it. I recommend mixing in some smaller goals to keep you feeling like things are moving forward.

If at first you fail, keep failing harder. I'm serious. The more you fail, the more you'll succeed. My fingers are crossed that this is sound advice, and that it will actually work. Charging headfirst into Suck Nation over and over will get you where you want to go. You can't get around this. There is no way over or under it. You must go through it. And closing your eyes and running blind isn't a good option, either. It's time to raise your hand up and say, "Hey Suck Nation, pick me!" There is no vaccine for failure. None of us know what we are doing at the start. The only way to update your operating system is to get into action and do it. Failure isn't so bad. I'm continually building up my resistance to failure by failing on the regular. My life is a comedic skit; each day is filled with material for laughing at myself. Whether the failure is a stepping stone or a reason to cry and feel defeated is up to me. Each time I come out the other side of a failure, I have a renewed vision that I wouldn't have been able to get any other way.

The other morning, it was raining and I was driving to our latest trial and error event—a month-long pop-up market in a beautiful space that almost nobody came to shop at. It was a four-weekend commitment—twelve shopping days. The entire thing felt like a bust. Once again I was trying my best and failing. It reminded me of our first market, one I've since tried to delete from my brain. In theory, the location had been ideal: it was in one of the busiest malls in the country, but there was no traffic for us. I'd been stressed for weeks about it and had convinced several people to help me to set up and work it. We didn't even make enough money to cover lunch. The experience was crushing. I had to tell myself the experience was good, like a fire drill. The only silver lining I could find was that we would never have our first market again. That was over. Dust your hands. I remind myself almost daily to have a positive attitude and that all of this is training me to play a bigger game.

I've had customers turn their nose up at our stuff and tell us what they think we should sell instead. And I've watched a man drag his wife into our booth and practically force her to get a sweat-

YOUR FEARS WILL GROW IN SIZE OVERNIGHT

shirt because he'd seen us before and loved what we stood for. You have to take the good with the bad. Nobody has it good all the time. I can work an event and sell next to nothing: the cheapest sticker pack and maybe a hat. Taking that hit with our time and the expenses to be there hurts. Then somewhere else, on a different day, with a different crowd, I might find everyone is jazzed up that Pony Friday is there. It's hard to crawl home after a dreadful show and think about attending another one. We count on that money, but worse, we rely on positive feedback to keep us going. Showing up at the wrong place is tough. And showing up when nobody knows you or cares about you feels shitty. It's hard being the new kid that nobody is sure they should be friends with. You're vulnerable. Being vulnerable sucks.

I design a lot of the stickers. I make the packaging. I stuff the Pony Friday sticker packs myself—and I staple them shut. This game is personal to me. It's not clear if it's more of a labour of love or an out-of-control creative fever, but it's personal.

Thou Shalt Not Drift

I'd rather not let life sweep me along. I'm not interested in drifting. The idea of floating aimlessly gives me anxiety. Slumps are choices that require a bit of action to get out of. By "a bit" of action, I mean a ton of little action steps all strung together. Move forward. Have a positive outlook. Stay on your creative path. Here are some of the strategies I use when I'm stucker than stuck:

- Shift your focus and step away from what you're doing.
- Go for a drive out of your environment.
- Take a long walk outside.
- Rearrange your space.
- Look for inspiration in books and magazines.
- See what other people are doing.
- Get off the computer and use a pencil.
- Call your mom—you should do that anyway.

Success is built one step at a time. If you know enough to start, your limitations can't hold you back from success. I know that if I don't face my fears today, they'll be back tomorrow. Fears don't get tired of showing up and taunting you—it's what they live for. And make no mistake, they're professional-level terror-builders and get stronger with every passing day. I recommend facing them now. Your today brain can't even fathom the person your tomorrow brain can create. It's time to make ambition your BFF. I've gotten this far and all I've been doing is making it up as I go. Remember that other people's limitations are not your limitations. Nobody knows the astonishing person you can become—*you* have to get out your own chisel and carve that version of you.

You Should Sit This One Out

It seems counterintuitive to take a break when you've got a deadline looming. There is no room in the schedule for a dog walk, slack lining in the yard or a glass of lemonade on your back deck. Yet it's the best way to get your mind out of the anxiety cloud. Sometimes a moment of doing nothing is the best thing for you.

There Is a Plethora of Great F Words

You can launch F-bombs in meetings as often as you like and it won't hurt you nearly as much as these three other devilish Fs: fear, failure and freelance. I respect fear but won't let it stop me. Failure has its upside. But it's freelance that's been a major thorn in my side, ever since I quit my full-time agency gig. Whenever someone labels me a freelancer or asks if I'm freelance, I bubble with rage. I don't need anger management, I swear. I'm just passionate about my business-owner mindset—and my overall life mindset.

I run my own business. I did have to freelance initially to keep up with my bills. Freelancers often work for multiple agencies and are still fed the same way as agency full-timers. I don't see Pony Friday as a temporary situation where I'm hustling for work while I figure out my life. The difference is slight but crucial. Owning your own company requires a new level of hustle. I think we all grasp that owning a business is something people take seriously. Being a business owner is legitimate and held in high regard by all. That other word is tricky. I've made up some definitions to help make my point.

Freelance is about grasping for crumbs. It's taking overflow work from other businesses. Let me further dissect it, and even break it in two: "free" and "lance." "Free" seems to imply that you don't have to pay for my creative services because it's a game to me and my contributions aren't worth a dollar value. True, I'm being negative. "Free" can also be associated with being free to do what you want, or the freedom from it all. You are free from the confines and structure of a full-time position, you are no longer a slave to your paycheque… or are you? In reality, most of us who quit full-time actually work all the time, or at least anytime someone needs us.

"Lance" makes me think of someone riding a pantomime horse with an oversized costume dagger, skipping around with the intent to impale. Not quite the medieval knight version that might have come to mind for you, yet still a good visual to associate with your business if you're the type of person who sees the world as a semi-ridiculous and cutthroat arena that doesn't have enough food for everyone. Yes, I want to impale that next project. (Personally, I think there is more than enough to go around. I have an abundance mentality.) So, maybe freelance means you've been released from captivity and are likely to be impaled.

YOUR DREAMS ARE GOING GOING GONE

There's a difference between doing freelance and owning a business. People interpret freelance to mean a variety of things, whatever suits their situation or values: jaded-rebel-that-barely-works-and-can't-make-ends-meet, or charges-whatever-they-want-and-spends-half-the-year-at-a-resort-on-the-beach. Freelancing has been known to be both. Your vision of freelance can set you up to fail. Think about that fun little side hustle where you drum up a few buckaroos here and there to pay for your vacations. Well, when you go into business for yourself, the word "freelance" can keep you thinking small. Are you small potatoes? I'm not. I'm big potatoes. I want large contracts, a big slice of the pie and a vision my business can grow into. I do take contracts, which you can't call freelance because they require relationship management. Big companies do multi-million-dollar contracts, and that's the way I like to see my business. So, do you run a business or a side hustle?

The Carrot They Dangle Is Rotten

If I could pass on advice to my younger self, I'd give her a pensive smile with a slightly furrowed brow and tell her how tough times were coming but she'll somehow manage to clamber through them. Once safely on the other side, she'll see it was worth the effort. None of the cover-your-eyes storms are permanent. The dust will settle and the view will be worth the effort of holding your ground.

Awards can play tricks on you. Getting my name on a silver lion and black pencil was simultaneously the highest high and the lowest low. I had bought into external validation hook, line and sinker. I was part of a herd hierarchy and doing well. I wanted to win awards and be accepted. It meant everything to me, until in a snap I realized it meant nothing. Rewards for high achievements feel great, but comparison kills and you have to be aware of that when you pursue it. Comparison is the worst. It snags my self-worth when I'm not prepared for it. You should never let your dream get in a competition with someone else's. Social channels make it tough to avoid. Here are some ways I compare myself to others:

* My weight and fitness level.
* My relationship and parental status.
* The places I haven't travelled to.
* My business revenue and personal income.

I frequently get suckered into the comparison trap for a whole list of things, but never for my dreams. My dreams belong to me, and that includes how I interpret my success and my trajectory. As an entrepreneur, it can be hard to watch other people run businesses that seem to be succeeding faster than yours. I find it frustrating to look up from my diligent work and see someone miles ahead—you may even be glancing up at me and feel I'm the one who's making it happen at an accelerated pace. We're all at different stages, going at different speeds, and creating different things. As common sense will remind us, it's a journey, not a race.

Remembering this doesn't mean you'll stay envy free. The pangs of jealousy are the same whether I'm watching others jet ahead or feeling the sting when I'm notified that a handful of individuals have unsubscribed from the Pony Friday email list. Along the way, we're all going to gain some and lose some. You have to continually pony up to play. Money is nice. I won't deny that. For a moment let's put the thought of cash aside and consider other things that do have the power to make you happy. Don't take my word for it. Take this lesson from all the grandpar-

RESPECT THE BOSS TITLE

ents out there. Our elders tell us that you can't take money with you. They know that the most valuable currency in life is time, and what you choose to do with that time is what's important. Many of us will reach our deathbeds with regrets about things we didn't do.

For a moment, think about all the ways you've been reckless with your time, then add to that all the ways you've neglected your dreams. Money comes and goes. Time only goes—and your dreams are a once-in-a-lifetime opportunity. I'm infinitely more concerned with what I do with my time than where I spend my money. One of my big wins was socks. Here are some other ways I'm killing it:

- I own my time and decide when I work.
- I have people who work for me that I actually pay.
- My career path is paved in creativity.
- The brand I built is all mine.
- I have a dog-hair-covered life from two Dalmatians.
- My reality is walking my dogs in the middle of a weekday.
- I'm basically role-model material to the core.

Comparison is the dark side of social media. You know, that black hole of scrolling that sucks you in and turns the dial on your mental state right over to sad and worthless. Maybe you haven't experienced it and I'm alone in this. Just imagine watching your friends eat your favourite kind of cake and you're not allowed to have any. When I find myself mindlessly pawing through posts, it can be a slippery slope. I can spiral downward—feeling worse and worse about myself, my business, my contribution and my general existence on earth. In those moments, I'll compare my dog-hair-covered-sweatpants reality to those perfectly curated vacation moments, which likely took sixty shots and twenty filters to get right. It's not rational, but it happens. The feeling rushes in swiftly—a mudslide of yuck. I have to shake it off and remind myself that I'm in the game. I'm a player. I'm a contender for the win. I start picturing the victory cake in my head again. I start imagining the taste of the icing and the sugar crystals dancing on my tongue. I start visualizing the award ceremony. I'm in the game. You're either a spectator or a player. And I highly recommend getting a spot in the ring, a chair at the table, a place on the court or a chance at bat. Play the game, don't sit out and watch—otherwise you're left to live vicariously through others. You'll never get a trophy on your mantel for that.

I'm No Boss Chicken Nugget

There's something about the term "boss babe" that completely undermines and diminishes a person's accomplishments. Ownership of your career and ownership of your life path are not small things. I want those of us who have achieved boss status to spread our arms in celebration and embrace the word "boss" without a disqualifier. Don't girl, chick or babe the boss. Cutesy names make it less than it is. We aren't five-year-olds playing dressup. We're doing it. Respect the boss title.

I would love to join in all the fun of the female business groups, but the cost of entry is too high. Checking my worth at the door with a #bossbabe is a definite no from me. Ask yourself how many times you've heard the terms "boss dude," "boss stallion," "boss hunk," "boy boss," "business stud" or "boy-preneur"? I never have. Men simply refer to themselves as bosses, entrepreneurs and CEOs. No cute hashtag. As isolating as my position seems to be compared to many other women, I know there are plenty of us silently building empires and owning our accomplishments. We know the world is challenging enough without cutting ourselves off at the knees with an insult to our life's work. So many women are selling themselves short by using destructive terms. Stop belittling each other. It's not cute. It's offensive. When I think about doing anything besides stepping into my own power and my own light, it feels wrong. Shirking back from my boss duties isn't an option. I just think about my nieces and the other women out there who are watching how life is lived. If I'm not going to be brave, what do you think the chances are that they will?

"Boss chicks," you've got to be kidding me—I'm here to get work done. You can consider my general mood to be a step-aside-men-because-I-have-definitely-got-this and my lack of a ball gown is a good indication that I'm perfectly capable of rolling up my own sleeves. There is no damsel in distress here.

I occasionally try it out, though. I once asked a man in my life if he would kindly check my oil and tire pressure before I headed out on a long road trip. He was so sweet about it and completely missed the point by offering to show me how. Oh dear, I know how. I just thought it was something he'd be into doing as a way to pitch in. Any one of you who is over-capable and generally overqualified knows

The Truth Will Set You Free

I once watched a pro golfer do a talk about her sport, complete with a set of clubs and a few golf swings, while wearing a dress and heels. I mean, get the fuck outta here—that's the furthest thing from proper form. I have no idea what she was thinking. Did the "pretty lady" pressure get to her before she went onstage? We need to push back on social constructs and refuse to bend so we can show up authentically.

how hard it is to get help. It's not that people don't want to help you, it's that they can't figure out how to help you—since you've got it taken care of, no matter what it is.

Some of my friends refer to "boss babe" culture as toxic femininity, which I previously didn't know was a term. And maybe that's what you call it when others take your accomplishments and double coat them in monotonous pink fondant to make them more appealing for the playroom tea party. We're adults, people, real-ass adults. I even had an awkward email with a colleague after they'd featured Pony Friday on their website and referred to us as "girls." I requested that they use a more age-appropriate term, and they said they thought using the words "women" or "ladies" just sounded weird. Well, you know what sounds weirder? Using the term "girls" to describe female adults.

Time to Upgrade to Boss Level

You don't have to be an employee. You can be the boss. You can quit and start your own career adventure that doesn't rely on waiting or begging for a promotion. Avoid shortchanging yourself by referring to yourself as a boss babe or boss chick. Instead, I recommend plain old boss or, if you need to embellish, maybe go for super-boss and throw in a power pose for good measure. As glamorous as super-boss sounds, and it sounds pretty heroic, being a boss does present more headaches than being an employee—especially if you're also the board of directors, the shareholder, the investor and one of the workers. I joke to close friends that I own a sweatshop and I work in it, which is in bad taste. Roll your eyes if you must, but I exaggerate to make a point. Figuring out what role I need to play first in any given moment is an ongoing challenge. What's more important: personal growth, merchandise development, giving feedback, bookkeeping or client work?

BOSS YOURSELF THE HELL UP

If you're starting a small business and it's just you, or you and a partner, then you'll be wearing plenty of hats. You get to be human resources, accounting, payroll, marketing, sales, maintenance, management and anything else that comes up. It's swiftly all on you, so be prepared for people to push your buttons and have an appropriate reaction ready. Continue to grow your boss mindset and own your decisions.

Reducing our accomplishments can fuel imposter syndrome. I'm not into imposter syndrome. There is only one Elise and nobody plays her better than me. Fuck imposter syndrome. This is your life, you're playing the starring role and you did not have to audition for it. Every move is your choice and every day you're the one starring and directing, so make it worth living. Maybe imposter syndrome and identity crises are the samesies? I have definitely questioned my own authority. My arrogance. My audacity for thinking I could have it better or different, that I could create the life I wanted. We should call this by what it really is. It's fear. That's the root emotion here. There's no need to have a fancy name for it. We're all just a bunch of scaredy-cats trying to strut around like lions. When you find yourself suffering from feelings of inadequacy, remember that the words you use influence the way you think and the confidence you project. You deserve to call yourself a b-o-s-s because you've earned it—and you need to see yourself there. You are that good—even if it's not yet paying all of your bills, or any of them. Boss yourself the hell up.

Hollywood stars and celebrities are expected to smile whenever they're in public. The world doesn't grasp how their millionaire lifestyles could possibly be as difficult as our ordinary lives. I feel a bit like that in a small way, that I somehow forfeited my right to complain when I became an entrepreneur. My friends don't want to hear about my struggles when I'm living the dream. On the outside it looks striking, but this machine is a lot of work. But the world is watching, so you might want to smile. There's an unwritten rule about that, you can't vent about the challenges of running your own business—unless they're also entrepreneurs. Entrepreneurs are living the dream—our own schedule, making money on our own terms, pursuing our passions—so when we're having a tough time, the last thing we should ever do is complain about it to a friend with a corporate job. It's not about faking it or hiding the struggle, it's about appreciating the perspective the outside world has. You did it! You're one of the brave few and they want to believe that all the risks you're taking are worth it. They want to believe in the possibility of their dreams by living through yours. It doesn't help to tell them you sometimes have doubts, and that you're on your knees hoping that by some miracle a cheque will arrive before someone cashes one of yours. Remember this: giving up is a lousy idea.

To all of you small business owners out there, please know that being an entrepreneur is a real job. The fact that you made it up does not make it any less of real a job; it just makes you a magician that can create something out of nothing. That ability is intimidating to others and makes them uneasy. I like to believe that Pony Friday and

I are on our way to greatness. Time will tell. History indicates that if you keep going, you're likely to succeed, eventually. Eventually is the sucky part, because it's so vague. Which is torture. But it's pretty hard to stop someone who is determined to make it. Unless death gets in the way. That could happen. Death is such a wild card.

Victims Are Crying All around You

To maintain an optimistic outlook on dream-chasing, you have to steer clear of anyone who has a victim mindset. The woe-is-me talk has the power to drag you right back to where you started, and you'll lose hard-earned ground fast. If you can't turn around and run from these people, you'll have to tune your ears to a more upbeat station. Feed your mind with only the best. What if you catch yourself acting the part of a victim? This one is trickier, since you can get defeated and slide right into a victimized outlook on life without even realizing it. You can be there for weeks before you have the awareness to call yourself on it. My mental talk is pretty telling at the top of a potentially hazardous victim slide:

- Are you kidding me right now?
- That was supposed to be mine.
- Everyone is out to get me.
- All my clients want discounts.
- Nobody appreciates my attention to detail.

My chest tightens as I read these out. I feel crushed thinking about the moments where I've thought these thoughts and felt these feelings. Honestly, it makes me cringe that I can be so negative, petty and weak. We all have ugly thoughts sometimes, and we have to do our best to show them the door as quickly as they enter—or, better yet, right when they start knocking to come in. We need to let them know they aren't welcome. Heck, we should get them to tell all of their negative friends that our mind is forever off limits. Restraining orders for all assholes.

This Castle Needs a Moat

I've built my personal boundaries so high there's no getting around them. Soft boundaries make me miserable: people can't know where they stand because the outer limit keeps shifting. I don't draw lines in the sand where the tide comes in—those need to be redrawn over and over. Nobody takes nonexistent borders seriously; I recommend building boundaries like seawalls that can withstand a lifetime's pounding of ocean waves. When other people run up against your boundaries, they should slam into a rock-like surface and not be able to make them budge.

Some Advice on That Advice

Turn inward once in a while and do some reflecting on your own thoughts. You know more than you think, and you can figure out the rest. The mentors I needed to talk with about growing my business and building my dream were hard to find. It's tough to connect with another hustling entrepreneur. Neither of you has the time, and when you do connect, chances are they'll be on the opposite end of the stick. You'll be on the upswing and them on the down, or vice versa, and it won't be easy to get them to see the vision you have from your angle.

The mindset I had in year two is different from today's in terms of where I look for advice. Growing your network is important and seeking help from experts is not the worst idea, but in the end it's you in your game of life alone, trying to run a business that makes sense to you. Through my experience, I've become smarter and noticed that a great number of "experts" are doling out predictable advice. I've paid thousands of dollars for assistance when I could have gotten more from an entrepreneurship for dumb-dumbs book. Fuck people and their un-tested theories. I'm a lot more discerning now about where my advice comes from. That philosophy of "don't take advice from anyone whose life you don't want" is a good one to follow. Looking for advice when you're desperate rarely leads to positive outcomes.

BAD ADVICE IS NOT CREATED EQUAL

People love to give advice, especially on marriage, babies and business. Fortunately for me, I've successfully avoided the first two and only have to deal with the third. Obviously, I've been cornered on topics one and two—I wasn't immune to advice in my previous life as a non-entrepreneur. I've been offered heaps of dating advice, relationship advice, why-I-should-be-married advice, when-to-have-a-baby advice, horsemanship advice, dog-mom advice and career advice. The vocalizations got louder and more diverse when I started my own business, because I started listening. Big mistake. People who have never owned their own business love to volunteer advice. What the heck is that about? As a new entrepreneur, I was so hungry for knowledge that I'd find myself drinking bad advice the way a dehydrated fern slurps water. You could sing this next bit to the tune of that sixties spider-guy cartoon:

Bad advice, bad advice, fills eager minds with dreadful plans.
Spins a lie, any size, grabs rookies 'n'—makes 'em cry.
Look out! Here comes some bad advice.

Bad advice is not created equal. Some advice might be the right thing for nine out of ten entrepreneurs, but not for you. Other advice can be classified as asinine, given without thought from an idiot source. The worst is when bad advice comes from someone you trust or respect and is delivered with confidence. This heavy-hitting advice can punch you right in the gut and confuse you. One such little recommendation that runs counter to my instincts can send me on a mental and emotional tailspin. Abruptly, all of my go-with-my-gut moments are in question. I don't know about you, but my gut has never been wrong. When you know something to be true for you, don't allow others to question your path.

I'm dead-set on not wholesaling Pony Friday merchandise. This is something I've known from day one, but it comes into question whenever I open myself up to a constructive chat about my limited cash flow. The garden hose of liquid gold has a kink in it somewhere that can't be located. The majority of brand manufacturers are looking to get their new products into distribution channels as fast as possible so that they don't have inventory sitting in warehouses. They want to make money quickly—that's the goal, so they wholesale. Success is then defined by how extensive your distribution network is. This works because producing larger volumes can offer great profit margins. And what if I don't want to wholesale? Not wanting what the masses want is hard for most to wrap their minds around. I don't want my stuff to be lost in among the clutter of a hodgepodge shop, or available anywhere other than from us. Mind-blowing, I know.

The numbskull advice-givers are sitting on the sidelines with extra energy to holler out what-they-would-do-if-they-were-you comments. When you find yourself at the point where this endless stream of tips serves as comic relief, you're in the right headspace. Seriously, you'll hear some funny bits. Here's a darling of an unsolicited tip I received: "You should make pony underwear. Then I would totally buy something from you." I was unprepared for this moment: a priceless tip, delivered by an unsupportive colleague. I replied with a non-committal "good to know." The list of things that have been suggested as additions to the Pony Friday inventory is pretty long. One time a businessman suggested ties, and I realized he was vocalizing a weird fantasy parallel universe that he'd briefly imagined; in *this* universe, I doubt he'd wear a Pony Friday tie if I supplied it.

When your ideas are criticized, you need to do your best to ignore the negativity. I know it hurts. I've felt the sting of the opinion bee many times, but it really has nothing to do with where you're at or where you're going. It's confusing to hear that someone would support your business... if only you made something they wanted. When I first experienced this passive-aggressive shopper-friend-asshole behaviour, I had the urge to kick them in the shin. One time I was working a booth and a lady said, "You should have socks for little kids," and I replied, "No, I shouldn't." And I meant it, but I should have kept that to myself instead of blurting it out. Yes, I could see these stranger braindumps as others feeling insecure and needing to make lame excuses on why they don't support my business, or dismiss it gently like a passing butterfly. An interesting thought and nothing more. Down the road, I won't bat an eye. (Who am I kidding? I'm sensitive when it comes to my creations.)

To be fair, there is good advice out there too. You generally have to dig pretty deep for it. The people with the best advice are those who are too busy hustling in their own entrepreneurial game to give you the time of day. They're the most genuine and the most helpful. More than that, they're compassionate and want you to succeed without having to stumble over the same things they did. These rare jewels will give it to you straight every time. One of the gems I heard early on was about a company that allowed you to put your parcel into USPS in Canada. It's genius. Now, I know of several businesses that offer this service across Canada, in most major centres. At the time, it was something I didn't even know to look for. You can't find what you don't know is out there.

You can also advise yourself. When I'm stuck, I ask myself what advice I'd give someone else in my situation. Pretending the advice is for someone else allows me to release my panic and be objective. It's so easy! Please picture me shaking my head, because it isn't easy. If I weren't physically, emotionally and financially invested, it would be easier to make a rational decision. It's important for me to consider if I can live with the outcome. Even indecision is a decision, and sometimes it's impossible to wait to collect more information before moving ahead. Decisions are power moves. The more decisive you can be, the more unstoppable you'll be. My advice: take your own advice first. Seize the next opportunity that shows up for you, and the one after that. And then repeat.

Most advice-givers are deficient. They simply vomit their fears at you so you can stay with them in Stuckville. Stuckville isn't far from Suckville; they're a twenty-minute drive apart and share the same kind of landscape and citizens.

Every bit of advice you get is coming from someone who isn't you. They don't have what you have. They don't have your drive, your talent, your ambition. They don't have your friends, your family, your connections or your gonna-get-this-done attitude. If you don't like what other people say, you have the right and the privilege to ignore their advice. I find this to be a simple and effective strategy. Plug your ears to advice.

Business Coaches Are Vampires

I'm unsure about business coaches in general—most can probably be scared off with garlic. The idea that one self-professed guru should be part of your decision-making team over the long term might work for a traditional business, but so far it hasn't worked for mine. What I have found is that they'll suck your blood (not literally) and your bank account (literally). My first business coach was good at putting me through the motions. Looking back, I assume he was regurgitating an online course or stuff someone else had said, while overcharging me. He wanted to make sense of my sales funnel, which I never understood. Here it is: the phone rings and I do work. The end. Oh, and I send them an invoice and I get paid. This "coach" stroked my ego more than was healthy, and he had no idea what he was doing. I should have scrutinized him better—he really had no real experience of his own. Like zip. Zero. Nada. It was so painful. If he were smart he would have told me that we weren't a good fit; instead, I had to fire him.

Do you remember when you realized that you were smarter than (or as smart as) your parents? That's going to be a recurring feeling along your entrepreneurial journey. You'll outgrow people you used to get advice from. Then you'll get a lot more discerning about who you engage in business conversations with.

Not to knock all coaches, because they can be more than worth it. If you get a good one, they'll help you see beyond what's in front of you to something bigger. They can help you see past the end of your nose and question your conclusions. Find other entrepreneurs to bounce your thoughts off and try to use them as accountability partners. You can also coach yourself. And you should. The advice you need to hear is usually not the advice you get. Remember that allowing your goals to be overly influenced by any one person, approach or method is risky.

JUST GO FOR BOLD AND ASK

The "Elise Method" is to put your head down and get to work. If you're doing stuff and being productive, it tends to get you further than talking about what you could do. You should know with complete confidence that every action and every step you are taking is moving you closer to where you want to go. Being a creative entrepreneur takes perseverance, just like anything else you want to achieve in life. Don't falter.

If watching a movie is more important to me than my creative passion, I can't expect to be in the same place along the path to my goals as someone who hustles for their art. But I do have to carefully balance work time with play time to ensure everything I do hums along in the fun zone. It's about balance and fitting in that needed time out to recharge and give my mind a break. Zoning out to a few seasons of a show doesn't get my business anywhere, but it can save my sanity.

If I die tomorrow, I want my eulogy to be something more than "she was a creative and she worked a lot." I tell people that I'm going to chase this dream to my grave and give it my last breath. And I truly hope that ends up being more than a slight exaggeration.

Whatever Pony Needs, Pony Gets

I'm passionate about achieving my dreams and when I think about how far I'm willing to go to get them, few things are out of the question. Would you take the shirt off someone's back? If you really needed it, would you?

Apparently, I would, and have, in a satire with the local garment factory related to sizing. I was smug about the fact that we had our shirts sewn locally. Our customers loved their soft-to-the-touch quality. This shift in manufacturing was a step in the right direction and it was time to order a new batch of sweatshirts. Reorders are simpler than gambling on a new supplier. And since we'd already had success and were ordering the same thing again, it should have been simple. We just wanted a couple of cover stitch amendments to an existing pattern, so we requested a sample. I messaged the request and learned that they were backed up. So backed up that they wouldn't be able to get to our order for a couple of months. Now, I was used to business hurdles, and I decided that was fine. I wasn't willing to go back to our old way of ordering shirt blanks from out-of-the-country suppliers to have our designs printed on garments that anyone could get.

In the meantime, the factory's head designer had quit and there was added confusion regarding the pattern we'd been using and the sizing. I'd sold out of shirts, and all I had for comparison was the Pony Friday sweatshirt in my wardrobe, faded from being worn and over-washed in my endless attempts to keep it dog-hair free. I'd also ripped the tag out when I took it from our inventory so it wouldn't get confused with a new one. So with the missing tag, and the fact that we use gender-neutral sizing, the only reference point was my memory and the belief that we had another, smaller size. I tried to recall the customers who'd purchased an extra-small and if I knew any of them well enough to borrow it back in an effort to solve this dilemma. Most of my connections simply aren't that tiny.

I swore my tired sweatshirt was a size small, and the factory was convinced it was an extra-small. And being someone who regularly fluctuates between sizes, it was possible. Yet, something in the back of my mind told me that it was in fact a small.

I drove over to confirm the pattern sizing and found that they'd made the prototype a size larger than I'd expected. I tried it on for fit and found myself swimming in fabric. What a sizing debacle. They'd made their small, and I argued that they'd sewn a medium. We were floundering. My brow furrowed with confusion as they pulled out printed pattern pages to show me that my shirt was an extra-small. I was living in a sitcom. This sort of moment should be funny, but it felt like there was so much on the line. I now had zero confidence in the sizing process and left the factory perplexed. As a company selling clothing, getting consistent sizing is a necessity. Imagine going to a store knowing you're a medium according to their size chart and suddenly you're a small. That type of experience is maddening. I needed to solve this.

To add to the confusion, we were getting additional sizes graded to be more inclusive to our customer base. I wanted our future size range to go all the way from extra-extra-small to extra-extra-large. We got a designer on board to grade a smaller pattern and were set to move ahead. Bewildered by my lapse in memory, I figured I must have been wrong and that my shirt must be an extra-small. Order approved for production.

The following week I was running errands and one of my stops included grabbing some holiday decorations from the roller skate shop where we'd had a pop-up the month before. Through some incredible serendipity, the petite-framed shop owner was wearing her Pony Friday sweatshirt, and it was clearly a full size smaller than the one from my closet. I could tell immediately that shirt would be skin-tight on me. A wave of anxiety rushed through me. I'd just approved the next order of sweatshirts with the factory and they were being cut and sewn.

As I lingered at the skate shop, chatting with the owner about her recent vacation, the new store layout and the upcoming roller dance lessons, I was bubbling into a frenzy of dread and contained hysteria. All I could do was stare at her shirt. It was the smaller size, the actual extra-small, the one the factory had convinced me had never existed. But it did, and one was here, right in front of my face. I excused myself and left to phone the factory. I sat in my vehicle, fingers crossed, hoping they were behind schedule, which was typical for them. I was informed that they'd already cut our shirt order, but none had been sewn. It was a miracle. That meant they didn't have sizing tags in yet and it was possible to divert this catastrophe.

How do you ask someone to give you the shirt they're wearing? A shirt they purchased from you. Picture this: you're at work and someone asks you to give them your shirt. When you come face-to-face with a moment and you need something that someone else has, you have to ask for it. I quickly explained my situation and made my request, promising to bring said shirt back in a jiff. She handed it over. I could have cried. Here was another entrepreneur, a comrade in battle, appreciating my predicament and doing whatever she could to help me. My heart filled with gratitude and I raced to the factory to remind them what size a Pony Friday extra-small truly was. This satire needed to come to an end.

I managed to return the lifesaving sweatshirt to the roller skate shop about an hour later and was thankful there were customers inside so I wouldn't go on and on about my gratitude and how monumental this moment was to me. I owe that woman a thank-you sweatshirt, which should be easy since I know her size. She saved my butt. To everyone out there saving butts in small ways, thank you. Thank you. Thank you. You make the world a better place.

To those of you who need the help, remember that you'll never get anything you don't have the guts to ask for. When other entrepreneurs make room to help each other, it makes a big difference; even the tiniest acts matter. We're all so busy hustling up our own dreams that when we lift our heads from what we're doing to contribute to the success of others, it's extraordinary. It's funny to me now that I once thought deciding what fabric colours to order would be my biggest challenge. We're all writing our own stories, seizing opportunities and pushing for what we need. The struggles are usually small. They're the little decisions you have to make and standards you have to uphold to keep your dream on the rails.

3

EMBRACE YOUR STRUGGLES

The Ivory Doesn't Want to Be Tickled

When I was twelve, I was in a piano recital. Cue the groans. I'm not a pianist, but my parents thought it'd be nice if I could play the piano. It's an impressive skill to have and I begrudgingly went along with it. Some of my friends also played, and it seemed like something parents who wanted cultured kids pushed for.

When it was my turn to perform at the recital, I went up and sat at the bench. I could feel all the eyes in the hall staring at me as I lifted my fingers and rested them silently on the keys. There was a gentle hum of tension flowing through my body, and each and every one of my digits trembled in fear. Being under the spotlight was not where I belonged—this piano recital was not my idea. Sitting still at the front of a room with hundreds of eyes on me wasn't a skill I'd mastered. My hands were shaking so badly that I couldn't play. The petrified-of-performing monster showed up and I allowed myself to be swallowed whole. I had stage fright. Tears started rolling down my cheeks. Scratch that, they were rocketing down my cheeks—I cried, because that's what twelve-year-olds do. No problem. I knew the piece by heart, so I didn't need to read the sheet music. My body was shaking so badly I couldn't get my fingers to make it through the intro. Where was my self-destruct button? That moment was unbearably long. All the eyes staring. All the thoughts of pity. All the whispers. The other kids had done fine. They'd done well. What was wrong with me? I felt stuck, unable to play with no way out.

In that moment, I made a pivotal decision. I rose from my seat. I told the audience and the adjudicator that I couldn't finish my piece. Yep, I was adulting at twelve. Thankfully, the adjudicator had compassion and commended me for not making them suffer through as I destroyed the entire piece.

I occasionally reflect back on that moment because it bothers me that I didn't push through the fear. Why didn't I? I've concluded that it was because I wasn't passionate about piano. It wasn't for me. When I think about the dreams that I want to pursue, I can push through that fear because they're *my* dreams—not something

MY INNER COMPASS HAS THE FINAL SAY

that somebody else wants me to do. We owe it to ourselves to fight through the nerves and anxiety blocking our dreams to get to the other side. Cats might have nine lives, but fear has 999,999,999—so about a billion. You can never eliminate it completely.

To overcome the fear gap, you have to face it and cross it. There are plenty of ways that I have held myself back in the past, ways I have since overcome. There were things that I ignored for years and got to later—everything has its time. At least it should. Ignoring things indefinitely that *need* to be addressed is a sure way to die from regret—or at least with it. I'm a writer who can't spell and has bad grammar. Nobody cares. I have six years of post-secondary and no degree. Nobody cares. I make my own luck. What I care about is uncovering all the ways that I'm still holding myself back and tackling them with the intensity of a two-hundred-pound professional linebacker. The more hurdles that I find and overcome, the more momentum I create to get over the next one.

My job is to get up every morning and annihilate my fear. I try not to waste time looking for reasons to quit, because those reasons always find me fast enough. There's no need to look. It's my job to bat away annoying reasons like mosquitos buzzing around my ears. If you aren't living for yourself, who are you living for? Truly. I'm living for me and you can deem that selfish if you must—I consider it the path of truth and personal enlightenment. I give my inner compass the final say. It's the reason I'm not married and don't have human children. It's why I find birthday parties for adults a waste of my time and social obligations things other people feel they have to do and not me. I only take on projects that I'm drawn to, with clients I have alignment with. And I'm quick to adjust my sails when the direction isn't working. You can fire clients. Being true to myself is better for everyone. It makes me happy, and when I'm happy other people want to be around me more—an undesirable outcome for someone who relishes spending as much time alone as I do.

Life Isn't Killing You—Your Choices Are

You need to figure out what's holding you back, break free from your patterns and get un-stuck. There are countless people who feel depressed—not chemically imbalanced depressed, just gloomy hearts that can't find their way out of feeling super bummed. It's beyond unfortunate. I've been a pessimistic maggot stuck on the same old miserable scrap of leftovers. Ruminating on a not-so-merry-go-round. It sucks. We're all going to die either way, so what matters is what we do in the meantime.

My first job in advertising put me in a negative state with a prisoner mindset. I had a wall calendar where I would cross off each passing day with a thick black marker as though I were locked in a cage. I had no idea when my parole hearing was, either—that would be the day I would quit. Meanwhile, I was stuck trying to sort out how I got to this awful place that I had mistakenly thought would be marvellous. How could things have gone so awry? I'm a creative. I went to post-secondary to get more creative and to be certified as a top-level creative, and I chose a creative career. And yet here I was feeling imprisoned in a cell (um, I mean cubicle), where I was doing what other people can only dream of, thinking of new ideas all day long. There were days I spent with my feet on my desk just thinking and getting paid for those thoughts. Why wasn't this making me happy? I'd done my ad schooling in the US, then taken a job in Canada while all my American friends were in the States working at well-known agencies. I convinced myself that this was why it sucked, and that if I were working as a creative in a US advertising agency with bigger budgets and on more glamorous brands that I would be happier. Those are the lies I told myself. There's no chance that would have been true. I know that now. I know that my happy is off running creatively wild on my own.

WORK HARD FOR THE CREATIVE MAGIC

Don't Forget to Breathe

How is your breathing? Dedicate some focus to it. I hold my breath when I'm learning. My horse-riding instructor takes on the task of reminding me to breathe when I'm trying to hone a new skill. I'll be concentrating so hard that I forget I need oxygen, and my horse gets busy worrying about what danger must be nearby, causing me to constrict my chest and hold my breath. Breath is simple and necessary. Few of us are experts, despite having done it our entire lives. "Just breathe," they say, as if it's that straightforward. Calm and steady is the best approach to major life changes, but sometimes my heart rate won't let me approach things that way. So I keep going, gasping for air as fast as I remember to get it. If you've seen any of my talks you might have noticed that I get a bit short on air from not taking enough of a pause between words to breathe. My vocal instructor has been teaching me how to take sips of air frequently instead of needing to gulp it down when I'm all out.

There Is No Last Call for Awesome

My inner critic and your inner critic need to shut up. Either that, or they should go head-to-head in a battle of the wickedest inner voice in the history of creativity. I'd be happy to set that up if I hadn't arrested my inner critic and locked it up in a dungeon somewhere east of I'm-not-listening-to-your-negativity-anymore island. Your best is plenty good enough. Make it your mission in life to celebrate the best you have to offer, and that best will continue to get better and better until you become the person you've been dreaming of becoming. You get to keep trying, and trying, and trying. You don't have to wait for someday to come around, you can make your someday today. Actually, scratch that—not only *can* you make your someday today, it's *time* to make your someday today. Why wait? You could be dead tomorrow. Mistakes give you wonderful lessons, and getting in over your head is the best place to start.

Let Laziness Hang with Other People

Success only looks lucky from the outside—nothing replaces hard work. You need to stop inventing excuses for yourself; they're a waste of time. I'm passionate about embracing the uncomfortable and getting comfortable with that squirmy wormy feeling. I have to fight for what I love and eliminate what's holding me back. Your dreams won't chase themselves, either. We all have to accept that hard work is the entire recipe. Four cups of focus, three tablespoons of determination, two teaspoons of resolve and a dash of try harder. Going back to bed is always an option—just don't make that choice

Fear Makes a Living
Wrecking Your Fantasies

If you have an idea to start a business, don't wait until tomorrow. Start in some small way today. Brainstorm all the ways it could work out. Think about the phenomenal opportunities it would bring you and the renewed sense of purpose you'd get. Take a step. If you're serious about making a life you love, you'll create the way.

too often. The I-tried-and-it-didn't-work-for-me attitude is quitter central. Magic doesn't work for you; you have to work for it.

Sometimes I need to bribe myself, but there's no shame in that. The magic is in the effort—settling is dangerous. When the carrot is dangled in my direction I work my butt off to get it. I'm a greyhound chasing a rabbit-stuffy lure around the track at top speed. I make myself crafty charts with rewards and sticker achievement levels, then watch as my productivity skyrockets. I've had achievement charts for writing this book, working out, walking my dogs, posting to social—all with different reward systems and varied incentives. New jeans, date to the waterpark, trip to the mountains. Figure out what motivator works for you and trick yourself. Make it a game.

I'm serious.

I Should Probably Do Laundry First

Call me a productive procrastinator. I run a tight ship. Bed made, dishes done, floors vacuumed, laundry washed, folded and put away. Dogs walked, supper made. And there's the mandatory petting of the dogs. Everything I do is something I should do, must do, need to do, like to do, want to do, have to do and choose to do. And when I fail to shift my priorities, I never get anywhere new in my business. The most dangerous part of being a productive procrastinator is that it's guilt-free. Occasionally, I'm hamster-wheeling myself to nowhere. I ruminate about conversations that are now irrelevant, under the guise that there is still something to learn from them. I volunteer to carpool to an event, adding over an hour of drive time. I postpone decisions because emailing feedback is suddenly too much work. I rummage through my desk drawers and recollect where I got certain knickknacks. A pen that changes its sassy saying when you click it. The notebook filled with never-gonna-happen ideas. That unicorn tape dispenser I got for Christmas and other random trinkets. We all need breaks and taking them is important. And then there's time wasting.

ASK FOR HELP UNTIL YOU GET IT

Time must be carved out to accomplish my dreams. There is no "extra time" in my life; I have to consciously choose one thing over another. I realize that some of things I've listed are not productive, but they are funny human habits. Ruminating gives me the willies. It's about trusting the decisions I make and pushing forward. We need to coach ourselves and know with complete confidence that every action and every step is taking us where we need to be. In the end you're the only one grading your "life as a human" report card and you're the one deciding which path gets the top marks and which one is a failing grade. I've always felt out of my element doing what everyone else was doing. Stepping off the beaten path and bushwhacking is where I feel at ease. When I'm on the same path as everyone else I feel constricted. And the moment I step off, I'm myself again.

Failure Gives You a Reference Point

Remember how I said that the first Pony Friday pop-up shop was a bust? And that I don't care because we'll never have our first again? The stress I carried going into that show was off the charts. And now I can consider it our fire drill; after that, we started to envision how we wanted to do things. The first talk I ever did I was standing in a packed room with over a hundred people. I had chills and was shaking in my shoes, but I was doing it. I was building fortitude for a more impressive future. We all have fears. It's about getting out of your own way and forging ahead. I regularly assess my life to see how I might be holding myself back. I can't sail across my ocean of fear if I have an anchor in the sand. My job is to do what I can with what I have from where I am. Pull up my anchor, lift my sails and cross my fingers that the wind cooperates. Most of the time the wind is some form of assistance needed from someone else. Keep asking for help until you get it. The universe will eventually show up.

Forget the Easy Way

When everything is falling into place, we call it "karma" and "luck" and we forget that we've earned our kismet. When fortune's on my side, I know I've been working hard and hitting all the whack-a-mole rodents. On the other hand, we have "easy," which is about taking the slacker's way out. It's calling for takeout instead of making a home-cooked meal. It's ordering the cheapest business cards you can and having them arrive on your front step in forty-eight hours. I cherish easy, his standards are low and he never judges me for any of my less-than-ambitious choices. Too bad selecting the easier option often leads to long-term pain, and the difficult option usually means things will be easier in the future. It's funny how that works. Sitting on the couch is easier now and if you do it too much your body will suffer down the road, while exercise is more arduous in the moment and you have everything to gain from it. Easy is lucky's lazy brother; he cuts corners. The thing about luck is that you have to earn it. If you want to hang out with luck you can't spend time with easy, it's that simple. Here are some signs you're taking the easy way out:

- It's a quick fix.
- You think of it as good enough.
- There is no sense of pride in it.
- You think of this as a one-off.
- It's not up to your own standards.
- You use the phrase "I guess."

Nobody is perfect, and even I slap things together once in a while. It pains me to tell you that, but I won't deny it. If you're doing something in a flash and you know deep down that if you were somehow setting an example you'd choose otherwise, take the time to do otherwise now. Regret is something we could all live without, so don't tolerate shoddy work.

Clarity Is the Opposite of Waffling

Or maybe ice cream is the opposite of waffling. I'm not sure, but business requires decisiveness. Boldly commit to one direction, then stay calm and keep heading that way. No running in circles. The ability to stay calm is crucial. Your clients are hard to find. Stay calm. Your product isn't selling. Stay calm. You're losing money. Stay calm. Your bank accounts are depleted. Stay calm. Change takes time. Your actions and decisions aren't going to bear fruit quickly. Choosing a new path requires letting go of the old and reaching out to take hold of the new. It's agonizing, but this is the kind of eradication that I crave and choose to embrace—the death of my past weaker self and the birth of a stronger, braver self. Obviously, this isn't about literally killing myself or being suicidal. Reincarnation might be a thing, but I'm not into testing that theory. This is about conquering fears and quieting your inner scaredy-cat.

Roll with It Like a Wobbly Wheel

I love change. Love it! It helps to chant that to yourself in the mirror when change is coming at you faster than you're ready for. My instinct is to resist change. That's human nature. I have to remind myself how great the adrenaline of change feels and how good it is for moving forward. Change is generally best when we initialize it and expect it. When it comes as a surprise, you may find yourself wanting to hide in the closet, hoping for the miracle of time reversal. Encountering things outside of my control is frustrating so it's too bad for me that it's pretty much ninety percent of life.

It's a Joke to Call Patience Hard

It does get easier to be patient as you get older, which makes no sense because you have less life left to waste waiting around. I want to witness change happening, and big changes are often a slow burn, hard to see. So in year four I cut off all my hair. Forcing change on myself lets me see that there's something happening. I could see less hair in the mirror, and so could everyone else.

Other people have struggled with my evolution, and I've surprised myself more than once since I became an entrepreneur. When you're changing quickly, you're too busy to send out a press release about it, and sometimes the people in your life need time to process. Shortly after my big chop, I ran into couple friends at an event. When the man realized it was me, he turned around and walked the other way. He simply couldn't deal with it. It was a bit odd, yet it made sense to me. (Unless he was being completely rude, thinking women should not have short hair—but we'll give him the benefit of the doubt since he has long hair and is likely emotionally attached to it.) I didn't even recognize my own reflection in the mirror for a month. It forced me to look at myself and reprogram my system to see that new image as me. You can't always force change in the direction you want things to go, but movement of any kind can be extremely helpful. Your soul needs you to evolve so you can bloom to your full potential. When you make a drastic move and take a bold step, however small, it ricochets. Chopping off a couple feet of hair in exchange for a super-short buzzed-in-the-back do was drastic. So drastic that it took a full forty-five minutes to convince my hairdresser that I wouldn't have a meltdown about it (since I'd had a minor anxiety attack when she'd given me bangs). Keeping yourself in a state of change is healthy. It positions you to be ready for almost anything. It's much easier to get someone to take out the trash when they're already vacuuming. Imagine trying to motivate that person off the couch to do something. Not easily done, so staying in a state of change is my way of being ready for change. Keep change normal and you'll learn to love it, like it or at least get used to it. And going beyond driving a new route to work or trying a new dish at a restaurant is ideal. This is how you water the seeds of inspiration.

> **YOUR DESIRE HAS TO OUTWEIGH YOUR FEAR**

I believe in doing a new thing every day—a small thing or a big one. And I'm not going to give you a lame list of ideas to nudge you, because you're better than that. Now, go make a change.

It Turns Out That You Can Buy Friends

The world is forever telling us to do what we love, but for that to happen your passion and desire have to outgrow your fear of failure. I didn't adopt a dog until I was thirty-one because of my lame excuses.

For one, I lived alone and it would be taxing to meet a dog's needs by myself. Two, I lived in a townhouse without a fenced yard and I would have to take this dog outside on a leash every time it needed to go out, which would be often. Finally, I live in Canada, so there is this season called winter, when dogs still have to go out. I was being a baby and let all these reasons hold me back instead of saying, "I see all the hurdles and I'm going to do this whole dog-owner-writer thing anyway."

Getting Turbo, my border collie cross, was the start of my pet-hair-covered existence. Having a trusty someone by your side makes everything in life that much better. Sure, being single and having

STAY THE COURSE

a dog adds complications. Turbo needed a routine with regular trips to the dog park. He had his own preferences and came with his fair share of poo-tastrophes, but he also brought his whole heart with him. Turbo and I were attached at the hip and went everywhere together. He loved learning new tricks and seized every opportunity to perform them, especially if there were treats involved. He was the type of dog that would put himself to bed at night and made sure you got up in the morning. He was also the kind of dog that would chase a herd of cattle for hours and swim after a duck down a river, forcing me to charge through thick underbrush along the bank, cursing his animal instincts.

After Turbo came a horse, then at thirty-three I started Pony Friday. It all happened pretty quickly and that fall I adopted a Dalmatian pup and named her Dalia. My thirties felt long and arduous, but looking back I can see how the pieces fell naturally into place once I anchored into the person I wanted to be. All it took was deciding to live my life on my own terms. Like a crack in the wall, it started small and grew until it split open.

Relationships have the power to derail us. Turbo died without warning while I was on vacation and his unexpected departure hit me hard. I didn't even know he had been sick. He fell ill one morning and after a rushed trip to the vet they discovered he was riddled with cancer, and my partner made the tough call to put him down. Who the fuck kills someone else's dog? That was my emotional reality. My rational side was grateful for the team of people who had the strength to make the call to euthanize my dog. I know that was the best decision for him. Turbo had hemangiosarcoma, which is a crazy name for some nasty internal cancer, and he was dying fast. He was in so much pain they gave him fentanyl. It would have been cruel to keep him alive until I could come home to say goodbye, or even to wait to consult me before euthanizing him. There is no way to prepare for this type of trauma.

In that moment nothing mattered. There was no point to any of this dream-building bullshit. One of the things I do well is to prioritize my creativity above all else. Yes, all else, but even I hit my limit when the hand I'm dealt seems shittier than shitty. In that moment, leaving the game looked appealing. I remember kneeling on the floor, crying next to Turbo's frozen body with Dalia by my side. I wanted her to understand that he wasn't coming home again and that it would just be us from now on. That was the same day I'd booked off in my calendar to make my slide deck for the conference I was scheduled to talk at in five days. That task now seemed hollow. I had no desire to ever leave home again. Ever.

Somehow I made it to that conference after rescheduling my flights so I would be gone the least amount of time possible. I credit that accomplishment to being in shock. There was another talk two weeks later that I pulled out of because I needed time to grieve. Grief is tricky and many people won't be there to support you in your heartache. People you called friends will be ill equipped and lack empathy, the emotion required to comfort someone with a broken heart.

I also reached out to a dog-loving business coach from my past. There is something to be said about having a network of people with varying backgrounds that you can reach out to when you need their particular brand of skills. This man is also a speaker with an affinity for animals, so getting advice from him on how to deal with the catastrophic loss of my best friend and still take the stage was a lifesaver. The most important three words in his email were: "Stay the course."

You Have to Earn Your Patience

I have a horse. A real living, breathing horse that lives at a stable twenty minutes from my house. He's fun, and a real pain in the butt. He taught me patience, the hard way. I had moved him to the stable close to my house so I could get out and ride him more. Plus, this place offered both indoor and outdoor riding arenas for us to play in, as well as trails nearby. This stable has indoor box stalls for horses and outdoor pastures, and my gelding would be in one of the outdoor pastures. Imagine an enormous stretch of land the size of four football fields; it's picturesque, with trees lining both sides and a river at the back. Visualize sixteen horses, including my own, all living in this beautiful place. Now imagine my horse, a beautiful dark brown Arab, racing around this grassy paradise full tilt, running away from me. He was one with the herd. Catching a horse that doesn't want to be caught in an open field with endless places to run is impossible. It becomes a lesson in waiting. Waiting until he's ready. Waiting until he's burned off some steam and starts avoiding you by hiding behind other horses. Circling other horses in a game of ring-around-the-pony can be pretty infuriating if you think you should have been trotting down the trail twenty minutes ago on your good steed. If you decide that what you're doing in that moment is exactly what you're supposed to be doing, then it can be pretty enjoyable.

I'M LIVING MY LIFE AT FULL TILT

It would take an hour to wait him out every time I went to see him the entire first summer he was at the new stable. I started planning time for it. I got exercise chasing him around the pasture, and I grew patience while finding the joy in the moments we spent together. It's a lot harder to stand up a person than a horse. Horses don't know when you're coming, but they can hold grudges. When I abandoned my expectations of what our time should be spent doing, it was easier. Instead of doing drills or worrying about lessons, we hung out. I'd sit on the fence by the river and watch him eat grass. We'd walk side-by-side down the dirt road, just spending time together, and I stopped seeing him as a horse and more of a friend. A teacher. His name is Fable and, as I said, sometimes he's a real pain in the butt.

IT WON'T
JUST
HAPPEN

Try Not to Overlook the Obvious

My sister was our second online shopper and she only bought a sticker, which I thought was super petty and weird. I had to ask her what her deal was and she informed me, "A lady needs a shopping cart." I'd forgotten to enable the website cart function, so she couldn't add anything else to her order. Oops.

Mistakes happen on the regular. Have you ever copied and pasted something and sent it to the wrong person? I hate group emails, so whenever I have to send something to many people, I either blind copy everyone or I send individual emails so I can use their names and personalize the message. And to make that more efficient I write one base email, then copy and paste it into separate emails, where occasionally I forget to correct the name it's being sent to. This one time I sent an email to Cathy that said, "Hi Jacqui." Thankfully Cathy is cool and said she liked her new exotic name, but I felt pretty foolish about it. Lesson learned, who cares. Nobody died.

I did it just the other day and sent a text to Jess that said, "Hey Carrie." I noticed my mistake and hastily added #saturdaybloopers to the message stream. And guess what? I'm going to do it again. Not that I'm planning to. It's simply that with the number of messages I send the odds are that it's bound to happen. Whenever there's a domino of bloopers, I know it's a sign that I'm moving too fast and I should slow the fuck down. It's comical that I consider myself to be fastidious. Mistakes are inefficient and there needs to be a balance between warp-speed and actually being effective.

Hello, Trust Fund Baby

I've got first-world problems by the truckload, but a safety deposit box filled with gold bricks isn't one of them. My backup plan involves moving back in with my parents. And I would recommend that any backup plan you have be just as unappealing.

Pony Friday is me—living my life at full tilt. My version of full tilt doesn't involve anything you might associate with someone else's full tilt. Nobody gave me money for this. I'm not a trust fund baby or someone who received a windfall. I have asked for money. The bank said no. My entrepreneurial parents have their money tied up in their own ventures and my friends shift their feet awkwardly when I talk about going financially all in. My life partner is risk averse, so they're not helping. They pretend not to hear me when I bring up subjects that make them uncomfortable—and me being broke is one of those topics.

Watching the revolving wheel of money in and money out is nauseating. I'm still at the point where I have to hustle up work to make money to pay the team building Pony Friday. There isn't a big wave of income so I pretty much pay to work. And my job is like owning a theme park, so maybe that's okay. One way I found a leg up was to move in with someone who didn't need me to pay any rent. I'm not saying you should throw caution to the wind and invest everything you've got into your dreams. Okay, I am saying that—but this is at your own risk. My money. My risk. Your money. Your risk. When I want something badly enough, I'll find a way to do it. I've surprised myself with how crafty I can be with my solutions. It's a splendid realization that no matter how many doors close I can always find another to knock on, or maybe an overlooked trapdoor in the floor to crawl through. Oh yeah, pay your bills. That's integrity, doing what you said you'd do. Follow through on that and pay the people you said you'd pay as soon as possible. Do it for karma.

I'm in trouble, but I've been here before. A few years in, I thought I was done—as in financially-maxed-out done—and I managed to get out of the hole in a month. Maxed out line of credit. Maxed out credit card. I keep pushing my limits and waiting to see if I'll make it through. Everything works out for me. I believe in that. I have no choice. Autopilot doesn't exist; I need to be alert and driving.

This place I'm in is familiar; I'm strapped for cash. How many months will this last? Pay the interest on the cards. Refinance my house, again. Try not to be fooled by closed doors or what appears to be the universal direction. There were ample moments when I could have called it off and not bet on myself.

SERIOUS CREATIVE OBSESSIONS AREN'T SIDE HUSTLES

I needed money. Money to buy inventory. Money to pay for help. Money for "capital investment." That's what the businesspeople call good old cash-oh-la. Lack of money is one of the million reasons why I can't do what I'm doing—why I can't build what I'm building, and why I have no business being in the business I'm in. Those million reasons don't matter because I'm doing it. Side hustles don't always work for passion projects. It's pretty hard to keep a creative obsession on the side if you're taking it seriously. Satisfying your creative appetite will likely take more than a part-time investment.

Who do you ask when you need money? Maybe you have rich relatives, won the lottery or have an illegal drug business on the side. That wasn't my reality and still isn't. The bank seemed to be a good place to start. They've known me for years. They store my money and I have a lifelong relationship with them.

Banks Can Be Bummers

For the purpose of this story, we'll describe the bank as an evil ogre. Now imagine this malicious brute tossing their head back with a wicked husky cackle at my request for a loan. A loan to grow my inventory, develop new product styles and promote Pony Friday to get necessary exposure. They wouldn't even take my soul in trade because they said it wasn't worth enough. Obviously, that's not exactly how it happened; however, it is how I felt. Belittled. A fly's pet flea being returned to the pound post-adoption because I "wasn't the right fit."

Let's rewind for a moment. I'm a pretty cool kid. I run my own show and by the time I approached the bank, I had accomplished a lot. And yet in the eyes of the snobby bank, I was a joke—and apparently that joke was not worth risking a small loan on. I was hoping for something in the low five figures. In business lending that's nothing. High rollers come in asking for a million bucks and they get it.

It's irritating when finance experts tell me that they want to help me and string me along when they likely knew from the moment I shared my business ideas that they weren't going to be able to do anything. It's a date with someone out of your league who only accepted because they were bored and had nothing else to do. I spent days scanning and collecting paperwork for them. I jumped through all the hoops. I think I even provided a DNA sample and a letter relinquishing my first-born child. (Slight exaggeration. No DNA sample was requested or given.)

This is what I heard: "Hey, cutie. We don't want to invest in your lemonade stand because we can't envision you being able to pay us back. It's adorable though. We wish you luck." Complete this with a condescending cheek-pinch and you're right there with me. None of this *literally* happened, it only felt that way. I suffer from childlike optimism when I don't want to take no for an answer. I just hear "keep trying" and it'll work out. So, I went back to see this macho bank a year later, thinking I was in a better position, having done so much more. Pony Friday was in a way better place. We had done a ton of work to grow the brand in that year.

I can't recall what the bank said verbatim, but I heard, "Oh, yes... lemonade-stand kid. I hear some people do enjoy lemonade, but we don't, so it's tough for us to imagine that as a viable business. Maybe it will happen but we highly doubt it and we're not willing to give you any money." Now, imagine them patting me on the head and sending me on my way. Another turned-up nose from them, along with the how and why of their decision that seemed intentionally complicated to confuse me. The bank wouldn't lend me money—yet offered me a business credit card. Um, okay.

That same year, I happened to be in a workshop with a financial analyst. This person's job is to help the lordly banks decide who should get money. They build intricate algorithms that numbers get plugged into to see if you should be lent money. It's more or less a fancy family tree of numbers. Numbers making number babies to determine if your business is financially viable for a loan. There's no heart and no vision. It's all based on what you can prove—and it leads me to think that if you can prove it in the numbers, chances are you probably don't need the bank's money. In reality, it's likely easier to get money if your business is not creative or called Pony Friday.

I asked for money again and got another no; yet that same week I received *another* offer of credit, this time in the form of a business line of credit. If people keep offering me money, I'm taking it. It gives me breathing room. This money lending system is so confusing. On another round, when the bank suggested they would like to help and that again I should collect a bunch of paperwork to send over, I knew better. I'm wiser. My time is worth too much for me to waste it searching for paperwork to scan knowing in my gut that the entire thing will be fruitless. I might as well dedicate my life to finding the power to spontaneously combust people at will. That would be an impressive skill. Ha! You've been incinerated. Okay, that was dark and I'm convinced the world is better without an evil Elise running around, so I'll stay the course on building my pony-positive business instead. Isn't it great when others treat you as though you're a three-year-old asking them to buy stock in your finger-painting art gallery? No. Nope. It. Is. Not.

What do you do about it? Feel hurt? I felt hurt. I probably went home, flopped on my bed and moped. I probably complained to my dogs about the encounter at the bank and squeezed my eyes shut hoping to open them in a new reality. And I did. I opened my eyes to the reality that I was more than capable of continuing onward without any assistance from the bank. I just didn't know what that looked like yet. So I did what I do best. I brainstormed some solutions. I could sell my vehicle—a nice cash influx, but completely unproductive for getting around. I needed enough money to get from point A to point B. I needed money to buy socks, but at that point I only needed money for the down payment, not the full cost of the order. Could I get that amount a bit lower from the supplier? Yes. I could. Instead of paying the usual fifty percent up front (which they required for new clients), they would accept forty percent, which was a critical win. Heck yes! I'm gonna eat these fries and pay for them later.

I could hustle up a bit more work and be craftier with my cash flow. Let's take a moment to acknowledge the term "cash flow." Dollar bills in motion. Sometimes they make me motion sick, but I get that damming the river won't help—I have to keep the current moving. The deposit I needed my client to pay on my next job could pay for the deposit on the socks, which would get me through the next thirty days. I started thinking in baby steps rather than leaps or even long strides. Instead of thinking yearly, monthly or weekly, I might think in terms of days or even hours. It's not always pretty or stress-free, but I trust it will line up.

Even today I'm thinking in steps. How much money do I need to get me through this month? I focus on that number and the rest is gravy. Even if it's just enough to pay the interest on my credit cards and my line of credit, it still inches me forward. And I believe that at some point things will tip in my favour—when you work diligently enough, they inevitably do. This often takes considerably longer than we'd prefer, but you can't sprint a marathon.

Living to my creative fullest takes risk. I've embraced the thin and tangled strand that holds my life together and threatens to fray at any moment. I imagine it as a thick rope suspended over a large gully that only the brave would dare swing on. Stepping off the ledge and into uncharted territory with no safety net below. It certainly makes life exhilarating. I'm the only person in the world who knows all the stress and anxiety I'm feeling. I've been doing what I fondly call financial acrobatics. I have no idea how the money side of things might come together. I might sound (and be) unsophisticated about my business balance sheet, but this is the name of the game. It's about how far I'm willing to stretch to get where I want to go.

YOU CAN'T SPRINT A MARATHON

I'm expanding my risk tolerance as a business owner, manager, creative director, speaker and investor all at once. Pony Friday doesn't have investors. It's just me bankrolling the entire thing with my savings, selling my stocks, re-mortgaging my townhouse, cashing out my mutual funds, selling my townhouse and flipping my vehicle to finance a newer one. Plus, my ability to hustle up more work, and finally secure one small little tiny business loan with a personal guarantee from me. If this is what they refer to as bootstrapping, I'm living it. Pony Friday exists through my hustle, my credit cards and turning my bank accounts inside out. My current goal is to keep shifting money around to keep it all moving forward one little step at a time. I've maxed out my personal credit card and my business credit card. There are times when I've felt proud of my financial stability and then equally embarrassed by my lack of funds. I was using a self-serve checkout the other day when my card was declined, and it wasn't a big deal until the employee at the kiosk hollered over to me, "Ma'am, your credit card was declined." Half the store heard and I had zero shame. I still don't. That was seriously unnecessary on their part though—karma's going to set that right. Shame on them!

I'm disclosing my piggy bank's dietary deficiencies in the hopes that you'll feel some solidarity in the risks that you're taking. Money isn't something people talk about, and that makes it feel humiliating when you don't have it. It's too early in the game to know if the chances I've taken so far were good or bad. What I do know is, I'm at peace with the decisions I made with the knowledge I had. I'd do it all over again because I'm in the game. I'm not on the sidelines watching someone else play. I have mud on my face and fight in my heart. Hanging on by a thread is still hanging on.

Dive into Conflict—You Belong There

One of my least favourite roles is debt collector. As a small business, getting paid is arguably the most important factor for your survival— if you've done work, you need to get paid, and the faster the better. Even before you've done any work, you should be taking a deposit. Are you one of those creative types who don't invoice on time (or ever) and then struggle to get paid? I get paid and you should too. Take it seriously. Playing debt collector is a drag, but I'm completely willing to transform myself into a pest if one of my clients doesn't pay on time.

I've heard more than a few varieties of excuses. They've told me the cheque was in the mail and I've told them that I'm completely willing to come and hang out in their lobby all day until they pay me. We need to get paid. There is no other option. I have to feed the pony. If I don't get paid, we go under. As a small business owner, I'm never on anyone's priority list. I get shoved to tomorrow's to-do list and forgotten about. The number of times I've had to follow up on these things to get them done is daunting, but then action happens. I follow up and we keep moving ahead. It's called willpower. I've succeeded in making clients sweat enough to same-day courier their payment to my door. The fundamental rule is that you didn't put them in that position, they did.

MAKE THEM COUGH UP YOUR MONEY

Clients will tell me they love my work and that it's getting higher results than anything else they've done—and in the same breath ask me to lower my rates. They don't want to pay them. Yes, I'll take that brand-new luxury sedan for the price of a used no-frills entry-level hatchback, please. The expectations are ridiculous and it's your job to manage them. Other clients have justified delays in paying me because they hadn't been paid yet by their client, but wait—that was never in our agreement. Yes, I do hope they get paid . . . except I don't really care, since it's not my problem. I've had clients try to weasel out of paying for things because a project went over the original scope and the extras were agreed to verbally. Thankfully, there were also emails. You need to document everything in a paper trail. Ideally, you'd capture everything in a signed contract, but if you need to add things later on, you'd best be writing the details down and emailing them over. Cover your butt and carbon-copy everyone.

I had a gloves-off fight with a suit once over an extra $700 in scope creep. It wasn't much money to them as a multi-million-dollar company, but it came down to how it was going to make the person overseeing the project look, since it had gone over budget. My advice is to hold the line. You did the work that they asked you to do, and there's no reason to volunteer to eat the entire overage—or even part of it. In the end, it all worked out and we were paid what we were owed, but the discussion to get there wasn't pretty. You aren't a volunteer. Fighting for $700 preps you to fight for $7,000 or even $70,000 or more.

It would be pretty silly if I really had to follow through and sit in someone's foyer waiting for a cheque. I don't have time for that, and have no idea what I would do to pass the time. I did show up at an office once and ask to talk to the owner. The owner wasn't there, of course, and instead I talked to the staff about the fact that Pony Friday had not been paid. It was awkward for everyone, but they had put me in that position. I did a good job on my end of the deal; all they had to do was pay me. As a small company, it's tough to pay my employees if the big fish that I help don't pay their end in a timely fashion. We need to get paid to pay others; it's the cycle of small business life.

If You're out of Money, Make a Trade

Your lack of cash flow might be a problem in need of a creative solution, and you can turn it into a game that you win. There are alternatives to money, you just need to find them. Pony Friday has been known to make trades.

We traded for our first photoshoot. Some photographers we met needed a more professional identity, so we made them a new logo and some business cards. No money for models? No problem. We asked our designers and photographers to recruit friends and family, and paid them in tank tops and t-shirts.

I've paid a contractor with travel points. Pony Friday needed some graphic design work and the designer wanted a trip for two to Vancouver. Trading for things you need makes good business sense as long as the trade works out. We've traded design services for accounting services a couple of times and it worked for a few years—until it didn't.

But traders beware: it doesn't always pan out. There's a reason we all trade money. Buyers typically get what they pay for. Traders? Not always. I've definitely ended up being stiffed on a few trades. Trade is usually a risk worth taking when you don't have much capital to leverage. We once created a logo design in exchange for a few weekends of retail space. That one didn't work out that well, since our investment was about ten times the value that we ended up getting back in trade, but you live and you learn. It's risky when you complete your side of the bargain first.

The craziest trade I ever agreed to was for cheese buns. We did some work for a local bakery and agreed to take gift cards as partial payment. Since the project was for their branding and signage, I figured I could share the love of baked goods with potential clients and send people to the bakery to see our new work and eat cheese buns. What? Too cheesy? Thankfully for our waistlines, that project got cancelled midway, and they had to pay us in regular money for what we'd done. It's a good idea to have a kill clause and know what will happen if a deal falls through. Make peace with the trade you made—it likely helped you in some way or you wouldn't have agreed to it. Not every trade will be monetarily equal, but as long as both sides feel that they are getting the value they need, you're golden. Chase those IOUs and cash them in. It's completely reasonable to ask the other party to pay you out instead of following through on a trade. Reality is always shifting and sometimes the trade no longer makes sense.

Stay smart about your trades and keep note of them for your own needs and to cover your butt. If you're a business, the government might take an interest in your trading ways. Big unrecorded trades could be viewed as a tax evasion strategy, which I'd be willing to bet is big-time frowned upon by mister tax collector. So, I'm in no way encouraging you to be shady with your taxes or do anything illegal. I'm not an accountant, a lawyer or a fancy number cruncher.

I simply like a good trade—I've been trading for years; I even traded for my horse. What's a horse worth? It depends on the horse. Mine cost me a place to live for a few months while a lady broke up with her significant other and got back on her feet. Another horse-related trade I made was for riding lessons. My instructor needed a brand and a website and I wanted help finessing my riding technique. Personal trades are obviously simpler than business trades, but there's room in the world for both.

Bang Your Head against the Wall

The number of decisions I have to make on a daily basis is crippling. I get decision fatigue. How did she die? "Death by a million micro decisions" isn't a great headline. My go-to solution has been to write whatever it is down on my to-do list and get to it later. This behaviour feels organizational, but it's more like classy procrastination. This bad habit puts things off and makes it easy to shove things down the list, essentially drowning them out with more pressing things—or worse, they get repeatedly moved from list to list in an exhausting game of hot potato until they're forgotten. There's always room to improve how I manage tasks and decisions. My top concern is usually three things, when it needs to be only one.

Some days I feel as though I'm juggling rabbits and they're multiplying faster than I can toss them back in the air. Not that I can juggle, which is probably the point. Priority is singular and even multiple priorities should be limited to less than a handful. I have a set of priorities, but I didn't always embrace them. Deep down I knew what I needed and wanted, yet somehow I'd get trapped in a not-quite-right situation, usually led by a desire to please others. Sure, I can volunteer for the bingo to help fundraise for your kid's school, since your husband can't do it. Yes, I can absolutely drive across the city to meet you for coffee for the sole purpose of you picking my brain about branding for free. Of course, I can babysit your bratty kid who will misbehave the entire night and not respect bedtime. Picture me raising my hands up and saying, "guilty." I'm guilty of getting distracted and doing things that aren't mine to do.

FIGHT TO STAY IN THE ZONE

Thankfully, I've stopped bending my needs for others. I deserve more. We all do. You do too.

Often, tiny decisions are simple. Giving feedback to a designer on a project. Responding to an email with a yes or no. Declining a lunch date. Simple, but not easy. One small decision, easy-peasy. Two, no problem. Three, I've got this. Four, five, seven, twelve, twenty... it's an avalanche. When it comes to feedback, all I need to do is focus on that task and provide clarity on what needs to be improved. It's not hard if I'm clear-headed, present and not overwhelmed with other things. Concentrating isn't terribly difficult. Unless you remember the stereotype that all creatives are disorganized multitaskers with attention deficit disorders. There might be truth in it—stereotypes don't invent themselves. And if in one day I have to apply to speak at a conference, apply for a market, stop at the garment factory to review a sample, order new fabric swatches, follow up with the silk screener, write a project estimate, walk my dogs and do laundry, suddenly any little task seems to carry the weight of a life-altering decision.

The solution. Do it now. Right this second. Do not pass go or collect $200. Do it as soon as earthly possible. If an email comes in with a task that I can do right this instant, I will. The worst thing that can happen is for it to end up on the list. If I don't email you back within a day, you can assume that the possibility of a response is dead.

Doing things immediately has made me late for meetings, but I still swear by it. The do-it-right-now habit keeps the creative energy in motion, which is absolutely necessary to preserve. It's hard to restart the beast when it stalls out. Heaven forbid the beast falls asleep due to neglect. Prodding it awake isn't something I ever want to have to do. Don't interrupt the flow. Not ever. Fight off anything that takes you out of the zone.

The Captain of This Ship Is Me

My shift from employee to creative-solo-boss has been anything but smooth. Employees don't have to think about how they're being paid or where the money is coming from or anything concerning cash flow. When I was an employee, I wasn't interested in doing my timesheets and had to be reminded to get them done, which I understand now to be a frustrating behaviour for anyone trying to complete payroll. As an entrepreneur and boss of a small business, I'm the person that has to sort out the logistics. Deciding how much money goes where is tricky. Then you have to decide who can work when and on what and for how long. I wear a lot of different hats, and many of them I don't wear well. I'm a creative. I like thinking up new ideas and bringing them to life.

Managing people without the support of other managers was much like removing the wool that covered my eyes. It's been rewarding and unpleasant. I'm not the best boss. I might never be exceptional at any form of management, but I'm committed to learning. At the end of year four, I had an ugly management blooper. This particular blooper happened in an email exchange.

The exchange is between myself and Designer One—my first official Pony Friday contributor. Here's the situation: I'm in charge of the budget and shifting money around so everyone gets paid, which stresses me out because we often need the same dollar to do two things. I take on contracts to make money so I can pay people to work on Pony Friday, and Designer One was simply helping get the things done that needed to get done. This behaviour should be intensely celebrated since the creatives who work with me are deeply invested in the progress Pony Friday makes. They want it to succeed as much as I do and you can't buy that kind of loyalty. Here's the gist of how it went sideways.

Designer One did work Designer Two was supposed to do without chatting with me first. So I got freaky about hours not being tradeable. Of course, neither Designer One nor Two could see what the big deal was because someone did the work and the quality was more than fine. The not-consulting-me part was the root issue for me since it caught me off guard and I felt like things were going rogue. Which led me to say something that made me want to immediately eat my words, but it was too late. The email was already sent with the line, "It's like you want to be paid every time you lift a finger." It was mean and petty. And, of course, they should be paid every time they lift a finger, they're employees—not favour fairies. We talked about the need to loop in "the one who pays" on everything first and we've had smooth sailing since.

Communication is important at all levels and keeping the right people informed at every turn is a delicate dance. Managing cash flow is currently the most challenging part of my life. I'm learning. Thankfully, we got through that blip. Boss fails where I'm not empathetic are rare, but they happen. Having an employee stepping up to get something done is ideal and looking for the silver lining in every situation is a skill. This wasn't the only roadblock I've slammed my face into, but it's still one I feel like a five-star turd about. Not that my designers are oblivious to our tight cash flow. They were doing their own conservation efforts and reusing paper by printing on the back of old printouts. What I didn't know was that the presentation deck I had printed off to take to a client meeting had an old presentation on the back. I didn't notice until I was sitting in a fancy boardroom at the top of a skyscraper downtown with three executives in front of me. That joke was on me.

As entrepreneurs, we do need to pay people to help; it's the only way to avoid wearing out your favours. Ask for help. Allow yourself to have help. But unless you've magically found another person who wants to chase the same dream, you need to pay for the help you get. Parting with your money can be challenging when you feel like you have a limited supply. Relax and lean into the discomfort; being tense about it will just make things worse. Don't believe me? Reread the above exchange and imagine how it would feel to say something unkind and have to eat your words. Mmmm, this humiliation is so delicious.

> **NOBODY KNOWS WHAT THEY'RE DOING**

You need helpers around you. Thankfully, plenty of people want to be part of something meaningful, so if you have a good brand getting help will be easier. Others will want to have a connection to what you're building. Asking can be hard. I sometimes need to get my friends to pitch in, and I'll thank them with merch and friend love. I've also had to ask friends of friends to help. How you ask is important, but so is the number of times you ask. You truly have to keep asking until your need is filled and then, depending on where that yes came from, you might need to accept different ways of doing things. I often catch myself wanting to correct the behaviour I'm seeing to my way of doing things. Whoa! Stop and check yourself. Just because it's not how *you* would do it doesn't mean there's anything wrong with it. In fact, there might be everything right with it and something worth learning.

Figure Out What Freedom Means for You

In January of year five there was a change in our business insurance policy, and I needed all of my contractors to either have their own business insurance or get paid as employees. Most freelancers don't have their own insurance coverage. Maybe it's because that would be taking themselves way too seriously, or maybe because it's pretty spendy. It was time to turn my contractors into employees, so I dove into the task of creating employee agreements. Ick. I had to put on my Super Boss pants to get the job done and source some help.

What are Super Boss pants? Super Boss pants are action-ready pants you wear when you need to ninja-kick anything coming at you. My pants are typically denim—usually a pair of classic blue jeans, except my current favourite pair is actually bright green. (Not fluorescent green, think road-sign green.) Anyway, that day I put on my Super Boss pants and reached out to six of my business owner friends and asked them if they would be so kind as to share their employee contracts with me. I received five generic copies of contracts—everything from a one-pager to a six-page document,

We Might Need That Later

I'm no stranger to maximizing usefulness. My mom used salvaged scraps from my dad's old work jeans to sew us cool denim shit. She's a talented woman and never liked to waste perfectly good material. Do you ever notice how parts of your pants will wear out completely and give way while other sections look brand new? I was raised to see this and programmed with the urge to find uses for that "perfectly good" material. My mom still has a closet full of scraps—I mean, perfectly good material from old shirts and pants. Some of it was actually inherited from my grandma. If I play my cards right, maybe someday that box of scraps will be passed on to me.

Hmmm... nature or nurture?

Was I born weird or raised that way?

Little bit of both.

Yes, a bit of both.

complete with spelling and legal errors. This was a boss eureka moment. They didn't know what they were doing, either. Nobody knows what they're doing: they're just doing their best and figuring it out as they go.

Working Alone Rocks My World

Some people have trouble working from home all alone, and it's certainly not for everyone. I know people who need the buzz of an office, which I find unpleasant and distracting. I end up eavesdropping on conversations I don't care about, listening to someone else's meal planning or relationship drama. You need to figure out what's right for you. I want to be able to choose when I need to be on and extroverted and when I can be lost in my own thoughts. What if you're somewhere in between desperately wanting to control your own schedule and needing to work with large groups with someone else telling you what to do and when to do it? I pepper my calendar with just the right amount of coffee dates to spice it up. Often these are entrepreneur networking dates with people I consider friends or potential new alliances. Anyone willing to have deep conversations about whatever subject crops up is my kind of person.

> BEING TENSE MAKES THINGS WORSE

My office is a happy place. It has two desks that sit next to one another, each facing the window. The walls on either side are painted magnetic chalkboard black, and while that sounds cool and looks great, the chalkboard isn't really functional because it's too porous to wipe off. Also, heads up—the magnetic paint took about four coats more than expected. The other two walls are Pony Friday blue and there's a giant foam-core Pony Friday logo on the wall to our backs. We use this backdrop for online videos. We're all about branding.

Say What You Mean to Say

The ability to clearly state what you think and what you want are important life skills. If you're quick on your feet and can cut through the garbage, you can move forward at a faster pace. When you can't articulate what you want, you look unprepared, incompetent and weak. Take this example of a client interaction I had early in my career: I was part of a creative team presenting ideas to a client for their next campaign. It wasn't rocket science and our ideas were on brief—meaning that they answered the client request. And this is what the client had to say back: "I don't like this." I was confused; everything we presented was solid, a perfectly suitable solution. So we asked for clarification. Was it the colour they didn't like? Was it the font? The image?

"I don't like this!" they repeated louder and slammed their hands flat against the table with every word. And each time we dug for insight, they repeated the phrase and gesture with increased intensity and volume. "*I don't like this!*" they raged, with their hands slamming down with more force.

We were working with our agency's biggest client. This new point of contact was clearly less experienced than the last one and lacked the ability to form a useful opinion. At the time, I was completely bewildered, but years later I can piece together what happened. They were in self-preservation mode. I've seen this behaviour many times since, in different forms. Thankfully, I'm now more prepared for it and it's an amusing part of the game. Ideally, you can weed these clients out before you ever take on a project with them, or you meet them where they're at. Whenever I get a client acting hostile or retreating in fear, it's time to pick up the phone for a quick chat. If they email me in a panic about being confused or things moving too fast, I generally call them up right away and remind them that we're on the same team and they're in control of the process. They hired me. Seize this time to talk about where the project is at and what their concerns are. You want to put this kind of fire out fast. Everyone wants to feel heard and understood.

One of the conundrums with a bigger client who is unable to form clear thoughts is the added layers of bureaucracy. Sometimes they're new and taking over a project currently in play. They get worried about presenting the work up the chain of command and overwhelmed by how it will make them look to their boss. That's an extra layer of unnecessary complication to get your ideas past and one of the toughest things about working in large agencies for large clients. When you have a smaller business, you're the decision maker dealing directly with other decision makers—boss to boss. I bet you know what I have to say about layered client relationships.

"I don't like this."

Small and nimble is ideal for making things happen. We have next to no bureaucracy, unless you consider the many personalities duking it out in my head trying to be heard like the ads screaming at you through your favourite social app.

I hate ads in my social feed as much as the next person, so I challenged my team to think of another way that we could get some needed exposure. The two parameters were to do it without spending any money and still target our best customers. It's pretty tough growing your business when you have limited funds and your network isn't nearly as big and influential as your ego wants to believe it is. So, we focused on what we did have. Thousands of pairs of socks and a giant cut-out of a pony. We merged them into a game called Free Sock Friday. This game is only played on random Fridays, and it gets our customers taking selfies with our pony for free socks. They tag us and our latest market location, then share the post on their social account to earn socks. It's fun. Their friends see the posts and we get organic reach to our customer's networks. Free Sock Friday is a game that gets people to play Pony Friday brand ambassador. It's pretty genius.

Hold the Line for All Creatives

When I'm stumped on how to run my business and what to charge, I often consider what a lawyer would do. They're highly specialized in their chosen field and I'm highly specialized in mine. They work hard and have a unique skillset. So do I, which, in short, means same-same.

Saying no to something beneath you or no to a budget that's too small helps the entire world of artists. We need to protect our community from being undervalued, and sticking to our professional worth reminds the world that our artistic skills have value.

"I'd rather sit on my couch and eat chips," I said. The words slid off my tongue. It was delightful, until I became aware of the silence on the other end of the line. I was on the phone with a potential client who had spent the past ten minutes talking me up, telling me how talented I was. Feeding my ego rarely gets you anywhere. I eat up the compliments quickly, knowing they'll likely be confiscated the moment I don't give you what you want in exchange for them. The silent arrangement being: compliments in exchange for a ridiculously insulting deal. I was praised for ten minutes to get me primed for the kill.

"You know, Elise, we value the creative you bring to the table and we'll compensate you more than fairly. It's our policy to give you a line of credit that you chip away at over time until it's used up. The hourly rate you specified is completely reasonable for us on future projects, however, this time we'll need you to do it for half of that since we've already negotiated that rate internally." It wasn't about the budget: it was about the hourly rate they needed me to work for and it was about half the rate I was charging. My conscious brain was caught in the witchery of ego massaging and it took my instincts to react. A simple "no, thank you" would have been fine. Or I could have said, "That won't work for me. Thank you." After which I could have hung up without leaving words jabbing their ears. The thing was, I meant it: I would rather sit on my couch and eat chips. I still mean it and I'm glad that I said it. People are always trying to manipulate others, and creatives are often caught in the crosshairs. It's insulting to me, and to my kind, and deserves an insulting response. Not that I'm advocating we all go on a tit-for-tat rampage. Living my best life is about protecting myself from the bullies out there. If they toss a grenade at me, they'd better expect to get something back.

Every year I've been in business, I've had some clients excited to work with me and then get sticker shock at my rates, while others happily pay them. You'll find it of no surprise that those who chose a cheaper option often wished they hadn't, and later needed someone to fix it, which ended up costing them more. You get what you pay for. I've stopped trying to reason with unreasonable people. The last time I had a discussion about my rates it was over when they said, "That's pretty steep." And the rate I gave them was five years old and I was overdue for an increase.

Dear people, cheaper usually means shittier.

You're Broken and You Suck

Running a business is best done with a body in impeccable form, which none of us possess. We suffer from tight necks, migraines, intestinal upsets, unexplained fatigue, chronic pain and injuries.

The spring before quitting my job and launching my business, I'd dislocated my shoulder. At the time, I hadn't given it much thought—other than in the moment that it happened, when it consumed all of my thoughts. I was playing recreation dodgeball, something I have no interest in but had agreed to be the necessary female addition so my friend's team wouldn't need to forfeit. I can't believe this is actually a rule.

Having watermelon-sized rubber balls whipped at me isn't appealing because I can only dodge—I'm incapable of whipping a ball. I watched a woman on the opposing team grab a ball and then stretch her arm out to her side to get leverage to whip it. It looked powerful and I decided to give it a try. Not recommended. I put everything I had into that arm whip. My entire shoulder went with my arm and I have no idea where the ball went, since I was engulfed in a wave of wooziness and temporarily lost my vision to the blood-glaze of black. That's not how I saw that going at all.

Destination Unknown

Have you ever heard of the word "coddiwomple"? My friend introduced me to the term—it describes persistent travel to a less than precise location. That perfectly articulates my entrepreneurial life, and it's fun to say. I coddiwomple. And by that I mean that I persistently zigzag, trying to achieve an unclear goal. Now you're as confused as I am about where I'm headed. Good. Welcome to the club. The place I'm headed is so fogged in, it can only be depicted as hazy. My heart seems to know the direction of the place I'm headed, but my brain isn't in the loop.

Then I was on a slow, six-year slide to a physically low point. My shoulder was loose and unpredictable. It popped out at the most inconvenient times, including in my sleep and one night after working a long market day at a comic expo in Edmonton. The show hadn't been going well and I was exhausted. It was day two of three and I was walking back to my vehicle chatting with my booth neighbour, who couldn't remember where he'd parked. My arms were full with bags carrying the remnants of my lunch, the payment devices and the cash box. It was cold and dark outside, and I was tired. About midway through the sea of cars, my booth neighbour continued straight and I cut left, weaving through the vehicles to reach mine, which was parked along the side against a chain-link fence. I do my best to park in the same spot every time I'm at a show to prevent losing track of where I parked. The last thing I want to do at the end of a long day is search for my ride home.

I don't think I was walking overly quickly, but I'm a fast walker so I may have been. My foot caught on something hard about shin height, and I stumbled to recover as I was catapulted toward a parked car. I was envisioning a painful face plant onto its silver hood—my stumbling feet doing their best to keep me afloat. Arms full of bags, the only appendage I could free was the arm attached to the unpredictable shoulder. It happened in a flash. I shot my right arm straight out and caught myself with my right hand on the edge of the hood where it curves down to the wheel well. Then, in an unfortunate chain of events, the pressure rippled from my planted hand up to my shoulder, which buckled, and I crumpled to the ground, stuff falling around me.

The clink of a cash box dropping is plenty loud enough to draw a crowd. A group gathered around me to see if I was okay. I was not okay. I was in shock. I was shaking and my shoulder wouldn't go back in. Fuck. I was stuck. Plus, I couldn't see because the blood-flood was back. I don't know how many people were there; my best guess would be maybe four or five. I recall a man's voice coaching me on how he'd witnessed his friend slip their shoulder back into its socket. He had no personal experience, nobody did. I was trying to stay calm so that nobody would come near me. I feared being touched in such a delicate state. Finally, my joint slipped back into place and I was able to stop shaking. I could see a little bit and my pride forced me to gather my things, mutter a feeble thanks and stand. I felt nauseated and unsteady. It had all happened in an instant. I imagine it was less than a minute. A moment later I was standing, and my booth neighbour sauntered up, laughing about how he'd been mistaken as to where he'd parked his truck. He was now headed the other way and had missed the entire thing. The world was oblivious to my shoulder crisis.

The people you want to be with you when you need them won't be. Those loving humans that you know well and trust can't always be there when you fall. You're going to have to rely on your own inner fortitude and the kindness of strangers to get you through. I'm so thankful to that group of faceless strangers that came to my aid that night. I might have passed out from the pain and I know they would have helped me had I not been able to get back up. You don't know the ways that other people are struggling. Human lives are complex and we cannot possibly fathom the hurdles others are jumping to be where they are and get where they're going, but the world is full of kindness: you just have to look for it—and provide it.

My shoulder surgery was that following spring—just before Pony Friday turned seven. That summer we had a trendy shipping container store that was open Friday to Sunday in an up-and-coming neighbourhood. There wasn't much else my less-than-able body could do, so I worked many of the shifts myself, including Fridays. My swearing off working Fridays had been a great exercise in boundary setting, and it had uncovered a better outlook on how to balance "me time" with work time. Now, my life balance and days off are all interwoven and I have supreme control over time—okay, I wish I truly had "supreme control over time," but I just have better control than I used to, and I'm working at gaining more control all the time.

Broke Does Not Mean Broken

Pushing your future to happen means stretching things to the max. And for the first time in my life, I had a cheque bounce, and then another. I saw NSF sprinkled throughout my online bank account and I decided it stands for Not So Fun. I moved my horse from the nearby stable to live too-far-to-ride-away with my parents. I couldn't ride him while recovering from shoulder surgery anyway, so I told myself it was no big deal. This was an upsetting decision made through rolling tears and a bounced cheque, but Fable loves it there.

My lines of credit got maxed out and so did my credit cards. I even got letters in the mail that started with "Your account is past due and requires your immediate attention." Yep. Welcome to my new reality. I put my townhouse up for sale and managed to sell it after a few months; it wasn't exactly a seller's market. I paid off some debt and my financial ship stopped rocking for a time. The powers that be increased my credit card limit again, and I've started to wonder why they would do that since my funds are clearly lacking. Apparently, my credit score is alluring, and I still accept. I'm investing in my future.

I want this future badly. So badly that I'm willing to beg, borrow and steal for it. I sold my full-suspension bike for cash flow and rolled coins that weren't mine, in a home-based piggy-bank heist, to cash in at the bank. Imagine a giant water bottle. The kind you might see sitting atop a water cooler. Now imagine that for the past five years or more, you'd been diligently saving all of your coins in it and filling it right to the top. That bottle would be so heavy and burdened with coins that it would be hard to move and a task to roll. Now imagine that while you were away, some asshole of a desperate entrepreneur went through the trouble of sorting and rolling it all to take to the bank. Imagine how angry you'd be. That was your money. Your savings—yours to spend how you want. Only you live with said desperate entrepreneur (that's me) and that desperation led to her draining your savings. Oh, and this was after you'd already given her a handout. I'm not proud of this. Desperate times call for desperate measures.

Maybe someday we can replace credit scores with karma scores. That way, if you're nice, you have access to better resources. I think this would make the world a better place. Not that I'd have the best karma score. It's an idea I thought of and wanted to toss it out there. Feel free to run with it. Also, while I'm improving weird systems, what if those airport body scanners scanned you for good vibes? A beam of colourful light in the form of a rainbow curtain that could screen out anyone who is rude or non-inclusive. That way, when you get on a plane, it would feel like you're going somewhere magical with all the shiny happy people.

Smothering Dampens the Flame

At my lowest points I never want coddling; instead, I need someone to remind me of my strengths, tell me they believe in me and encourage me to dig deep. I used to play competitive soccer and my superpowers were endurance and speed. My position was centre midfield, where I had the best access to the entire pitch to support the team. It was my job to catch breakaways. Somewhere deep down I always had extra energy and another gear to shift into. I remember once, near the end of an exhausting game, our opponents sliced through our defensive line, who were panting up at the halfway mark. I was suddenly on the clock, but I felt too tired to charge back. I was running as fast as I thought I could when my coach yelled from the sidelines: "You're faster than that." And right then something in my brain unlocked a missing gear, and off I went with turbo-boosters, easily overtaking my opponent. It's incredible how much we're leaving in our reserve tank when we think we're giving it our all.

The faster you go, the more impact each step has on your joints, and it was on such a breakaway that I tore one of the main stabilizing ligaments in my knee. It was only a partial tear so it left me with an unstable joint that would slip out at the worst of times. Yes, it's as gross as it sounds and equally painful. Injuries force us to evaluate our choices and how we spend our time—whether we want to keep pushing our bodies in certain ways or whether we want to invent new ways to push ourselves. I was in love with soccer, and even after surgery I got back up and played for a couple of seasons to show myself that I could. But deep down I knew that path was over for me. Soccer and I had to part ways. Sometimes outside circumstances force our dreams to evolve and it's important not to spend too long mourning the loss of what could have been.

You Will Burn Out

Isn't that a nice and encouraging way to start? You will burn out. We all do at times. Burnout is normal, so be prepared to deal with it. (I've started planning ahead to mitigate the burnout.) I highly recommend naps. Late nights are what little kids think they want, and adults should know better. I'm too sensible for late nights. I'm a cross between a child and an old person (I suppose we all are) and I sleep a lot. If I stay up late, then I have to look for other ways to meet my sleep quota. If I'm tired during the day, I have a nap—or rather, I'm forced to take a nap. I'm not a napper by choice; I'm a your-body-is-shutting-down-now-so-you-better-just-accept-it type. In the middle of the day, when I've been told "no" one too many times and the struggle is too much, sometimes I have to sleep it off. This mysterious cure-all is my body's remedy of choice.

My body brought this to my attention one afternoon while I was out walking the dogs. Suddenly, my legs turned to slush and I feared that I'd spill over on someone's lawn with a pathetic slosh-style landing and not be able to get up. It's like when your phone battery dies—it goes from you-have-enough-juice-to-make-this-call to nice-try-sucker-I-am-done-here. I made it home without splattering on a random patch of grass and crashed immediately for several hours. After that, I started watching myself more carefully. There'll be burnout warning signs, but they could be subtle and easy to overlook. It's your job to recognize them for what they are. The signs might not make sense. I know a man who briefly lost his ability to see due to stress. And other entrepreneurs who've worked themselves at an insane pace and forgot to eat so they ended up collapsing and being hospitalized. When it boils right down to it, our health is all we have. My health is my first-place priority; it's the silent priority that trumps my other priorities. You know… my top three things are actually four. It's a tower of priorities.

Getting back to my sudden need to nap—if I worked in an office for someone else, this would not go over well. Imagine me turning

Pity Parties Don't Need Guests

When you find yourself feeling miserable, you need a plan in place to act on. There's no time to be indulging in this behaviour. If you can't snap yourself out of it, you need to know someone who can. Years ago, I was hanging out with my sister and droning on about this horrible relationship that I was in. She reached over and flicked me like I was a crumb on the table or a fly on her sleeve. It wasn't a gentle brush of her hand; it was a sharp one-finger flick. Point made. Shut up. We've heard enough. Delivered all in one well-timed flick. My circle isn't into humouring vocal ruminations.

to a boardroom full of coworkers and saying, "Sorry peeps, I'm just going to sleep off this bad meeting where you all shit on my ideas."

Being well rested is the best ammunition to fight for what you want. You're more resilient, you're more patient, you're more calculated and you're way better at finding the right angle to get what you desire. It's also great for your immune system. Call it a mission, duty or passion—pampering yourself is your burden. It's not my partner's obligation to guess my feelings or know when I need chocolate, stat. It's my job to take care of my own needs. If I'm miserable, that's on me, because I'm a fully capable adult. I'm not serving the world when I put myself last, and neither are you. Ending up in the hospital due to some stress-induced illness would be frightening for any of us. Dedicating daily micro increments of kindness to yourself is your responsibility.

I don't often take a full day off. There's too much I want to accomplish, so I weave "me time" in throughout my days and weeks. Dog walking is an Elise activity because I love walking. My body is an idea-making machine that needs continual upkeep to perform at the desired pace. That means a ton of sleep, a significant amount of alone time and daily dog walks. Walking is magic. Call it moving meditation if you want. It's healthy, enjoyable and you can do it anywhere at any age. With dogs, it's a no-brainer, but I walked plenty before I had dogs. Getting dogs didn't force a new habit—they just gave me company on long strolls. It's how I keep a clear head and shake off the anxieties of the day. People have been walking since the dawn of time, and it seems like fewer people do it on the regular than they used to. Being in motion is key. I walk. I always have. Always will. My grandpa is closing in on ninety and he still takes brisk walks every day. I've cracked problems while riding my horse, pedalling my bike, doodling, dancing—and even while driving on the highway.

Looking after your own needs will keep you from becoming crabby. I'm guilty of becoming hangry and that's never a good look. When I listen to my body, the world around me improves. Three years ago, a no hangovers rule led me to a dry year, and that's turning into a dry life. I don't have time for booze, and not drinking means I don't get invited out to drink—something that's usually done at night while I'm in bed. Double yay!

I'm not going to tell you what shows I binge-watch or how many hours per week I spend mindlessly staring at screens. I also won't tell you that you shouldn't, because I live in the real world and I believe in variety. Every now and then your brain needs to veg, whether that's colouring, painting, staring at a wall or picking scabs on your knee. The non-stop entrepreneur hustle is the reason many entrepreneurs

I know have suffered from digestion issues, adrenal fatigue or some other unexplained health crisis. You didn't start your business to run your body into the ground. Forced bed rest wasn't part of the plan. Finding yourself incapacitated will lead you to re-evaluate your entire life. So I think you should give your life a big re-evaluation first before any shit hits the fan. Nobody will ever have your back the way you do.

Shuffle Your Cards and Learn to Deal

Occasionally, I'm a panicker. You know, the adrenaline charged, rapid breathing, ruminating and sweaty-palms stuff—moments when you feel pressured, clueless, unskilled and out of your depth. My skin starts to itch and I squirm in my seat as my body gets tantrum ready. How do you deal with that kind of feeling? My lame answer: it depends. Sometimes I need to sleep it off, run it off, walk it off, shake it off, horse ride it off, cry it off, scream it off or (my former favourite) rant it off. Having a good rant buddy in your pocket is a must for situations that need to be storm-talked off your chest. The one thing I never do in a panic is snooze it. And I definitely would never perma-snooze it. No shoving it under the rug or suppressing emotions. No way. That's a ridiculous strategy that stops you from moving on. It's a part of my constitution. The repercussions for not abiding by my own codes are living a life of anguish and disappointment. If the situation involves another human (which it often does), I must phone them or meet to talk it out—fight it out and just get it done. No vague texts or passive-aggressive emails. Get this sorted on the double.

Another resurrected favourite is to dance it off, something I did a lot as a teenager. Even petting an animal can help. Quick tip: If I need to make an important decision in a short amount of time, I take a dog walk first. I can find at least an hour to do a gut check. Walking releases stress and allows my mind space to get another perspective on the situation. If you don't have a dog or time for a walk, find something else to take your mind off things—fold laundry, doodle in a notebook or do some light stretching. Playing on your phone will not help. Here are a few more ways to keep panic and other emotional shit at bay:

- Don't be a sucker when people stroke your ego.
- Never put anyone's wants ahead of your own.
- Bring enthusiasm with you or don't go.
- Do your stuff first and do it every day.
- Tell people how you really feel.
- Follow your dream—your life depends on it.

Ranting is my former favourite because I recently discovered that I'd gained a new superpower: I can now simply dissolve my angst. It might just be my new non-stick force field—you should probably get one. The next time someone asks you what superpower you would choose, forget flying or being invisible—controlling your emotions is the pinnacle of all powers. I'm certain I developed this out of necessity; there were fewer and fewer people who understood my rants. It's true, being an entrepreneur can be isolating, and I needed to develop new skills for my shifting environment. One of them is lessening the need to lean on others. I doubt it's possible to eliminate that need entirely; someone still has to deal with your body after you die. Call the morgue, pick out a casket, arrange the funeral—even if you get cremated and don't want any fanfare, there are plenty of people involved.

Here's what I do with my panic feelings now. I identify where it's coming from, which is hard since you have to be in tune with your own emotional health. Then I push the tension externally, where it came from. Most tension belongs with someone else. Then I think about what rant I would have had in the past, label the situation as unnecessary to replay and move on. The maturity that comes with being in your forties is magnificent.

My To-Do List Is Quicksand

Not doing something when I first get the opportunity is a waterslide straight to despair. Yippee! Misery, here I come. Hey, not so fast, because whatever it is, I'm going to do it now. And I recommend you reserve the shotgun seat for this approach. Take a moment, if you must. We can't hop to it all, every single time. So decide when you'll get it done and don't change your mind. Other tricks that work for me are powering through the most import-ant tasks before lunch, breaking large projects into smaller assignments, blocking off time in my calendar to do it another day and giving myself pregame pep talks. One of the ways I stay on top of all the moving pieces is to write myself little notes. Notes of encouragement on mirrors can do wonders. That way, when you see your-self, you also see a positive affirmation. Digital reminders are useful, but a paper trail means I can see everything at a quick glance. I adore sticky notes and aim to always be well stocked in a variety of colours. It's ideal to keep them handy, along with a thick black marker. Everything goes on a sticky note in black marker. If it's not on a sticky, it's not important, not happening, irrelevant, unnecessary and ignorable.

"PONY GROWS WHEN I DO"

Shame, Shame, You're to Blame

To achieve top-rated adulting, you should stop blaming other people for anything negative. I'm mature, so I blame my parents for every-thing, including my belief that anything and everything is possible. They told me that I am a blend of their extremes—they never elabo-rated on what those extremes were, and I think the only thing to do is assume the best and the worst of it all. I am extremely ambitious, extremely stubborn—ain't that a double-edged sword—dedicated, opinionated, passionate, hardworking, silly, fun, strong, capable and enthusiastic. I lucked out in the solid family department.

Nope, That Sounds Awful

As a rule, I don't do things I don't want to do. It makes me miserable, along with everyone around me. One of my rules is to not participate in anything that doesn't need my help. For example, our house needed a new washer and dryer. My partner asked me for my input and tried to lure me into going to the store to look at machines. I responded with a firm "that's a one-person job." That chore only needed one adult human to complete, so my tagging along would be a poor use of time. What were we going to do—discuss wash cycles for hours and do research on the best models together as we quizzed the salesperson? Barf. I beg you to stop double doing things. Just because you're capable and would do a great job does not mean you should waste your time on it. And don't fool yourself into thinking that arguing over stainless steel drums is quality time.

I grew up in a middle-class family of five with two determined entrepreneurial parents who built a business together to create the kind of life they wanted. Growing up with an inside view of what running your own show looks like, it's no wonder that none of us kids thought being an entrepreneur was a great idea. Or at least, that's the assumption I'm making based on the amount of time we've all spent working for other people. We saw our cousins and friends get nicer Christmas presents purchased by parents with corporate jobs. I heard about them going to magical theme parks with princess palaces and world-famous movie studios. And I seriously doubt they wore any hand-me-downs from their cousins. My parents had different priorities from those of my friends' parents. They felt Christmas was over-commercialized and they had no interest in spending money on those sorts of things. They put their money toward other stuff that as a kid was hard to wrap my mind around.

Our first big out-of-the-country trip was to Hawaii, not some overly-hyped-mouse-centric kingdom—a decision I couldn't make sense of at the time. As an adult, I can. We all make choices about what's right for us. My parents didn't follow what everyone else was doing. They don't care about trends or the pull of the herd and I'm thankful they passed that along to me. My siblings and I were raised to make our own choices and be true to what we as individuals believe, not to float along with the crowd. Pushback causes trouble in structured school settings and workplaces, but it's great when you're a creative entrepreneur.

Pep Talk Yourself

I struggle in ways that claw at my self-worth and have me questioning my abilities. I will feel weighed down with the knowledge of what could have been but isn't. And that thought will go in the failure file in my brain and validate my thoughts of incompetence. We need to validate ourselves in positive ways:

- Elise, that was over-the-top awesome.
- Hey self, you rock my world.
- Talk about a job well-er-than-just-done.
- More proof the sky is the limit for us.
- I'm more than enough; I'm awesome.
- Perfection, meet done-ville-fection.
- Time to call your momma and brag.

No Shoes, No Plan, No Problem

Not too long ago, I found myself barefoot at the animal emergency centre. It was 11:19 on Sunday morning and I still had bedhead—I hadn't gotten around to getting dressed yet. My plan had been to lounge around until noon before getting organized to tear down a market that was ending that night and pack for another one that was happening the next day. It was so nice out. The dogs and I had been wandering in and out of the house with the doors open; it was the perfect rejuvenation day.

Then Dalia had a seizure. I'd never seen anyone have a seizure in real life. It all happened in a blur and I went from thinking maybe she'd been stung by a bee to thinking she could be choking and was turning blue. I was perplexed and trying not to panic. I wrapped my arms around her with my fists under her ribs and attempted to heave whatever might be stuck in her airway out, then I reached down her throat to try to dislodge what might be there, knowing I risked pushing the object even farther down. Was she breathing? I couldn't tell. What if she died right here, right now? Fuck. Losing another dog wasn't an option. Fuck you, universe!

I was home alone and wondered if I should run out front into the street for help. Sunday afternoons are usually quiet, but I remembered seeing the new neighbours outside across the back alley. I hauled Dalia out the back fence and hollered, "I need your help." My neighbours came pronto. They reassured me that Dalia was breathing and I knew I needed to get her to the vet. I asked them if I could

Cry Me a River or Two

You're allowed to cry. We should exercise our right to cry more often. I firmly believe that the people who keep their emotions all bottled up inside are more likely to get sick and stay sick. Crying never hurt anyone—unless you're waterfall-crying while driving. Don't do that. You won't be able to see and you could seriously hurt someone. My mother always pipes up when she thinks my waterworks have gone on long enough. So, to keep her happy, we won't let a batch of tears derail our day. Meltdowns can be quite draining so those should be avoided, but give yourself some time to grieve. Dead ideas need eulogies. We're allowed to grieve dead people, getting dumped, ripped dresses and spilled milk. And we should be allowed to weep over ideas that will never see the light of day or those we thought were aces, but society wasn't ready for. Release the sadness. Let go of your could haves, should haves and why didn't I do that sooners. Shed a tear, even if it's just one. A nice solo tear will do you good.

ditch them with a five-month-old puppy and hauled ass with Dalia to my truck. I was pulling off our street when it occurred to me that I'd just left my puppy with people whose names I didn't know, the doors of my house unlocked, while wearing leggings covered in dog hair and driving barefoot. I didn't have time to grab my shoes or dignity—this was an emergency.

On the drive to the vet, I told myself that I'd done everything I could and kept glancing in the back seat to ensure Dalia was still with me. She'd mostly recovered in the fifteen minutes it took us to get to emergency, where I admitted her for observation and tests. While I was waiting, I called my other neighbour and she went to my house and introduced herself to the puppy's insta-caregivers, locked up my house and took Dante home with her. Talk about living among heroes. My neighbours are the best and I'm usually so consumed by my own shit that I don't make enough time to get to know them better.

The vet came out and invited me back to talk about Dalia. My first thought was: *I have no shoes.* So I said, "I have no shoes, can I come to the back like this?" The vet asked me if I had any shoes to put on and I said I didn't, so off we went to the back. I felt like I was in an absurd dream, and kept thinking how weird it was that people need shoes when Dalia had just gone back there barefoot. Dogs live their lives barefoot.

There are always people crying at pet emerge, but no one else was barefoot. I cried every time the vet asked me something. It was uncontrollable. "Tell me what happened," was followed up with a box of tissues for me—the vet also took one. "Dalia is beautiful," they said. Cue me bursting into tears. This was the same place Turbo died four months earlier. I was fuming at all forms of higher spiritual power. Dalia was not for the taking. What kind of cruel trick was this? I was having none of it. Pause the Elise movie and edit this scene pronto!

I did manage to gather myself and conquer the remainder of my day. I still had to tear down that market and make it happen the next morning at the other market. It seems like I'm always dismantling something or setting it up, the endless whirlwind. There's a little tornado hidden inside while the outside of my life can look a lot more stress-free and glamorous than it really is.

Thankfully, Dalia recovered and is doing great. Dante is happily chewing everything. I still have two dogs and a growing network of incredible people pitching in to help hold my life together. There are plenty of moments behind the scenes where shit hits the fan and you have to pull as many hands on deck as you can find to keep things from falling apart. Emergencies are a great way to get to know your neighbours, but being friendly and introducing yourself before you need help is always preferred. Lucky for me, the teens next door like to play dog nanny.

5

BEHAVE BOLDLY OR BE DULL

Pony Needs My Personal Growth

My business relies on my ability to step up and face the next challenge. Challenges that seem to fly at me faster and faster all the time, as though they're being shot out of an automatic pitching machine set on high. One of my greatest assets is that I can fear something and do it anyway. I'm not sure if that's courage or stupidity, but I want to be a living example for other creatives for stepping out of stability to find a happier version of themselves. Pony pushes me to create a stronger version of myself and gives me stamina to fight my self-doubt and push back on society. I'm dragging my current reality closer to my goal every day.

I have no idea where Pony Friday will take me. The tree that grows never looks the same as the seed you plant—this whole thing is an adventure. I have to grow for Pony to grow. I used to take every "no" from a stranger at face value and now I know to push back and ask questions. There was a holiday sale we wanted to be part of when we were first getting going and the only spots left were for artists.

Event organizers often mistake Pony Friday as a much bigger company than it is because of our branding, which often feels like the only thing we've done right. When we applied, they told us we didn't qualify as an artist and they wouldn't be able to accommodate us. I was determined to get in so I did some digging and it turns out that besides the handmade artistry items, they also allowed authors to set up in the same section. Similar to authors, we design our things and have someone else make and print it. With a compelling argument, I turned that no into a yes.

Treat Your Brand Like Royalty

Well-designed brands are powerful and can get you places you could never go on your own. I've lost count of how many yeses I've gotten because the Pony Friday brand is so solid. It's like having a cool older brother or sister bring you along to a party you'd never be invited to. A well-designed brand will command attention and get you noticed. Beyond good products, services and referrals, it's your branding that makes you attractive and memorable. It sets you apart. It's how the world will come to know you and growing that identity gives you power in much the same way your own reputation does as a person. Having a certain look in how you dress starts to become part of your brand. You'll grow your credibility through consistent actions and behaviours. There are people who know me as Elise, the woman with red hair, and have no idea that I'm a creative entrepreneur. There are others who know the Pony Friday brand and aren't aware that it's my business. They also don't give two hoots about who the owner is and from where I'm seated, that's ideal.

STRATEGY NEEDS ACTION TO WORK

Great brands can open doors you can't. They can take you on trips to do talks at creative conferences in places like Raleigh, North

Carolina. That event team was impressive and helped me solidify my path as a speaker. I didn't even have a reel or a video of me delivering a talk to send as proof that I wasn't a hack. They flew me out without any evidence that I could give a speech because they loved Pony Friday. Pony Friday opened that door for me. Nobody gets into a conference the way I did. Nobody but me—there's always an exception.

I submitted my speaker proposal to a bunch of conferences before I'd had much experience talking. At that point, I'd officially only done one talk and I was behaving boldly, sending out applications to speak. I was telling the universe what I wanted and it answered—a conference said yes. It's rare for anyone to apply through a website and get selected to speak. Generally, conference organizers are reaching out to the speakers they want to have on their stage and find speakers based on their reputation. I didn't fit the criteria, but exceptions happen all the time. All you need is one yes to move to the next level. The right application at the right moment to the right person and lickety-split I was an international speaker. This happened because of Pony Friday. I wasn't your average speaker: I was the creative mastermind behind an irresistibly charming brand.

It helps to have an edge that nobody else has. The only advantage I have over you or anyone else in the room is based on what I can bring with me. The majority of speakers have spoken on hundreds of stages, run seminars and have at least one book. I can't compete with their street cred. There is only one me. There is only one you. How you leverage that is your call and having another angle helps. I'm playing this game with a golden bargaining chip, because I built one. I built a brand that catches attention and makes others want to know more.

Your brand is your currency and it's worth spending time and money to supercharge it. Models are paid well, but supermodels rake in millions. Same goes for low-end car brands versus luxury brands. The latter spends considerably more on their product and brand experience, and their product and prices reflect that. Every brand has values and Pony Friday is no different. I pride myself in being the brand police. Many businesses get this wrong because they overlook the importance and potential value of their brand. Having good branding sets you apart and communicates what standard you deliver.

When you look at a brand, it's similar to looking at a person: you can see how they're dressed, their body language, and you immediately get a sense of whether or not you trust them. My friends know that I speak my mind. They can count on me to follow through on the things I say I will do and they can count on my honesty. Pony Friday and I have overlapping values, but we aren't the same. The brand has come to life in all sorts of fun ways, including bold apparel. What's best is that the Pony Friday brand, through its reputation, has opened a ton of doors that I would not have been able to open on my own. Two years later I went back to Raleigh and spoke at that same conference again.

COMMIT TO SLOW AND STEADY

It's easy to confuse what you would do with how your brand should act. These two things are not the same. As a small business owner, it's easy to mix up how you would speak and communicate as a person with the voice of your brand. Entrepreneurs are often muddled in how to help their brands grow. What we personally like isn't necessarily the best foot forward for our business. After working as an ad creative for over a decade, winning awards and helping other brands stand out from their competition, Pony Friday became my real-life case study for brand building. I already had a personal brand and I was setting out to build a business brand. (When you die, your personal brand dies, but you can sell a brand you built from scratch that doesn't revolve around you.) Now, firmly in shoes like my clients, I can tell you that separating yourself and your instincts on how you should behave as a person from your brand takes awareness. I'm a brand ambassador for Pony Friday. I'm the founder, the creative director and many other things, but I am not Pony Friday. I curate the brand. It's not me. Pony Friday is its own entity with its own perspective and personality. Maintaining that separation takes skill.

You might be in the same position I am—responsible for growing a brand. Even the self-declared brand police herself can get it wrong sometimes, so it helps to have a team. A team, even if it's small and scattered, can help steer the brand ship. I remember posting a blog image that wasn't well aligned with how we typically treat our graphics, and I heard about it. My secret is to keep training my team to hone their critical eye so that they will also spot inconsistencies.

Brand building is comparable to growing mutual funds. With mutual funds, you're encouraged to make regular investments over time and keep investing through market ups and downs. Start early and be patient. This is exactly how you should build your brand. Start with a little investment and build on that in good times and bad times; just keep adding to it and it will continue to grow. Some years it will seem to sprout rapidly and other years it may seem to stagnate. You have to trust the process and hand your concerns over to time. Commit to slow and steady.

People Will Try to Spend Your Time

Clients love meetings about meetings. But I protect the precious commodity of my time. Otherwise, it will no longer be mine; it will belong to someone else. Remember to build and maintain your boundaries. I find that when I set expectations on how I interact and use my time, people tend to sort themselves out. They're either with me, or they aren't. If you lived with me and walked into my office while I was on a roll, I would look up and firmly say, "out, out, out" until you backed away and out of my space. There are times when I cannot have others or their energy in my room—even my dogs know the word "out" and have heard it a lot. I need to safeguard my creative space, particularly when I'm in the zone. It's okay to turn off your phone and not check your emails for hours. Ideally, we would all get to wake up when our body wanted to, and the majority of days I get to do that. Some of the choices I make aren't exactly crowd pleasers.

Keep Growing or Wilt and Die

Personal growth should be a forever commitment. You must be steadfast on self-improvement. I've realized along the way that I wanted to have a brand that was bold and inclusive. My gender diverse friends taught me that it's not really possible to maintain a safe space; even if you want to, you can't. Their suggestion was to create *brave* spaces where people could be themselves. There's so much power in brave spaces and I want Pony Friday to create inclusive brave spaces wherever we go. I set a goal to only carry gender-neutral sizes for our clothing, rather than men's and women's. One challenge with that goal is socks, which follow shoe sizing. In Europe, they have a considerably simpler way of sizing footwear: it's based on the length of your foot and has nothing to do with your gender. In North America, we default to the US standard of men's sized shoes and women's sized shoes. We're in the process of creating our own translation of sock sizing to meet our gender-neutral needs.

I've trained the people in my world to be efficient. Even in my business, I don't get that many emails and my phone rarely rings. I've done such a great job of defending my time that others appreciate that we're only going to discuss what we need to discuss and keep small talk to a minimum. Outside of my entrepreneurial hustle, I make time for myself, my animals, my extended family and a select number of friends—I'm not a completely self-centred pain in the butt, more of an everyday pain in the butt. I only have time for the tiny inner circle and don't leave room for many social gatherings. That's my reality—and what's necessary to move my life closer to my dreams.

Pick Up Your Tools and Work

Unless you're chatting with the reaper about your exit (and I'll assume that you're not) there's still time to build the life you want. Creating your legacy starts with decisions about what you are willing to tolerate. As creatives and entrepreneurs, we need to protect our time and remember that not everything is meant for us. What's important, fulfilling and fun to one person might be a complete waste of time for us. We follow and unfollow accounts at alarming rates, but maybe we shouldn't have followed them in the first place.

Content is being churned out by the second and many of us mindlessly share videos and articles we haven't even read. I've done it at least once myself in my personal feed. I took a quick scan to see if was worth sharing and off it went to my followers, and I moved on to something else, forgetting that moment ever happened. My friend called me on it; apparently it was off brand for me. We keep Pony Friday's content original and creating our own stuff is overwhelming. Churning things out for a few likes makes us wonder why we're doing it all. The never-ending demand for things to fill your feed is insane and it's increasingly difficult to decide what's worth reading and what isn't. Start reclaiming your life—your inactions often matter more than your actions. I could still be a dog-less dud working for someone else. So if I'm boring you right now, move on. Make the time to design the life you want.

Momentum Is Your Business Partner

You might see me do something and think, *That's easy for Elise*. You saw it happen, but you didn't see the prep it took. You don't know how hard it might have been for me. I don't let hard stop me, but that doesn't mean there isn't struggle or tears. Everything I want in life is hard and scary for me, but some things can't be chased. Remember my horse? I had to meet him where he was at, and I think money behaves the same way. My interactions with Fable aren't always how I imagine they will go. Horses tend to teach you what you need to learn, much like money. Fable has taught me many things, including

USE YOUR INSTINCTS AS YOUR COMPASS

the fact that I'm not in absolute control of my life. I need to meet my entrepreneurial odyssey where it's at and not force it to be something it isn't. Holding a gentle perspective on life allows room for it to bloom in unexpected ways. It's dismal to think of how small my life would be if I didn't continue to fertilize it and give it ample room to grow. I refuse to chase money. I'll just keep showing up and hope that someday it starts to follow me. I'm always working to close the gap between knowing what I need to do and doing it.

Back when I worked at the agency, there was a long, drawn-out meeting where I had to explain the same thing multiple times, and I felt drained at the end. There were too many cooks in the kitchen and as I was leaving the meeting, one of the men asked if we could schedule another one about what we'd just talked about for two hours. I said no. There was no need to set aside more time to talk about what we just talked about. These are professional talkers: they just talk and talk and get nothing done. It frustrated me that while my hours for creative development on a project were being cut, there was an influx of staff eager to talk about strategy. Strategy only works if you put it into action.

I'm an action person who was surrounded by people discussing the pros and cons. They're trapped with their possibility nuances and endless theories about taking action, yet never commit to making a move. I find the entire thing perplexing. The talkers aren't the doers. You know some of these types too. Keeping one foot in discomfort is the ideal equilibrium to perpetuate forward motion. Where you put your time and attention will become your reality. Don't talk big. Act big. Be big.

If you're incompetent at something that you're not even interested in, you should stop doing it. Ditch the things that make you tired and run-down. Don't zone out, zone in. Focus on the things you want to do and get help with the other things that need to be done. Consistently doing things that drain you will empty the fuel reserves you need to get to the next level in life. When I'm concentrating on a task that interests me, it gets done with pride and joy. There is nothing begrudging about it. Your life need not be filled with resentment.

Ask Yourself What You Do Have

If I focused on the fact that I didn't have any money to grow a business, then I wouldn't be where I am today. I kept asking how I could take the next step in creating the life I wanted. What small action could I take to move an inch forward?

Tackling anything new requires a little bravery. You have to find courage within your core and believe in yourself. This can be difficult. Still, it's important to stop dabbling. Dabbling feels to me like poking something with a stick. Maybe it's a slug oozing past on the ground and you have the urge to touch it with your finger—but you have second thoughts and instead you nudge it with a small twig, which does nothing to satisfy your curiosity about touching the slug.

Go for it. You're a dream-chaser. Pick that slug up in your hands and get slug slime all over you so you can't hide what you've done.

We Forget to Take Our Own Advice

As adults, we learn to suppress our instinct to leave people who are bad for us and jobs that suck. We're conditioned to defy our own internal compass. As a culture, we override our instincts and drive them right into a bottle of antidepressants. What if instead we cried out and demanded that life fill our needs? I think life would listen and rise to the occasion—it has for me. I'm no different from you. I'm not smarter or brighter or more destined for greatness. I'm not even braver. I simply trust my instincts and act accordingly. My instincts are my compass. If you don't feel you deserve it, you'll never have it. Nobody will deliver it to your door. Dream central headquarters doesn't have a website with a twenty-four-hour free delivery policy.

I choose to follow my instincts. Each. And. Every. Time. Trusting your inner knowing when there are so many fingers pointing the other direction isn't easy. At the end of the day, when I'm lying in my bed trying to get a good night's sleep, the only thing with me is my truth. I'm the one that has to deal with the mental anguish of not following my instincts. My instincts look after me, so I respect them. I'm not about to break trust with myself.

The world says, "Go right."

My friends say, "Go right."

My family says, "Go right."

Common logic says, "Go right."

My instincts say, "Go left."

Going with my intuition calms my heart. It reminds me that my feelings matter. I go against the recommendations of my peers, my family, my mentors, my coaches, my accountants and my friends. I watch as they shake their heads. "You've lost your focus," they say. "You've lost your path." "You've lost your way." They wait, holding their breath, as they watch me go the "wrong" way. They think I'm headed off a cliff to an untimely death. They want to protect me. They want to keep me within the safety of the known path. But I know that's not where I belong.

There Is Power in Making a Decision

My mom taught me to be decisive. She's been drilling this into me for years. I remember a time in my early twenties when I was dating someone new and an old someone came to my door pining for me. I was conflicted. At the time, I was living at home with my parents, so this might have become a hot topic—or at least I thought it would. My mom isn't into hot topics. She is into smooth sailing and doesn't have time for drama. Want to know how she handled it in the most effective and least dramatic way possible? It stuck with me. We were in the kitchen—because everything happens in the kitchen—and she said nothing in response to my conundrum. Not a peep. She grabbed a small notepad and a pencil. Then, with the pad placed on the counter in front of me, she wrote one name on one piece of paper and one name on another. She let the pieces of paper sit there for a moment and then she picked up the old flame's name, crumpled it up and tossed it in the trash. Then she went back to cooking supper. Done. Nothing more to say.

One Foot in Front of the Other

I'm willing to step into unknown territory rather than stay where I know I'm not fulfilled. Pushing through what you know without all the information is preferable to gathering data that may not be useful while you stick around somewhere that sucks. Abandon the idea that you must have a plan. Needing to have a plan can keep you at a standstill. Find a way to move ahead with only a vague idea of your direction. Forward motion is king. When I make a big step, the first thing I feel is a wave of excitement and adrenaline, followed rapidly by fear and self-doubt and a feeling that I should go back to my comfort zone where I knew everything.

My future is a haze of unknown and that sometimes sends me into a ruminating panic. I'd love a glimpse at what's coming. A peek at where I'll be in five years, ten years or even twenty. It would be nice to see a movie trailer with some highlights of what's to come. Instead, I'm left putting one foot in front of the other, doing one seemingly insignificant task after another, trying to move forward to my best self. Not knowing much makes for gruelling work. It helps to focus on what I do know. And as my business ages and evolves, I have a better idea of what we should do in the next twelve months, since I can reference what we did last year.

Technically, I Couldn't Afford Any of This

Credit card interest is killer, but the alternative is a dream-chasing deficit and that's nearly impossible to recover from. Life charges interest on unfulfilled dreams, which is why you feel so burdened and weighed down when you aren't actively chasing them. When you put that lens on it, it makes that shitty credit card interest bearable. Everyone always says to do the stuff you're passionate about on the side, but I say the opposite. And I now have more than seven years with Pony Friday—peaks and valleys and plateaus.

Here's a breakdown of the highlights as I experienced them—correlated into human years for humour and perspective. This is an overview of my general business state, my personal state and my financial state. Break out the party snacks.

Year One: I finally found the courage to quit and not look back. Pony Friday is a summer baby, born July 13, 2012. He enjoyed an intrepid first twelve months as an infant and was, thankfully, crawling and diaper free. All I had was the name Pony Friday and the knowledge of what I didn't want. My business cards were cheap and I didn't have a logo so I used a random font as a wordmark—a creative embarrassment. I cobbled together a website and my business was live. Fortunately, I had a solid reputation in the local advertising world and contract work kept finding me. I'd work Monday through Thursday. I refused to work Fridays. Yes, I owned my job, but I was still working for "the man" (albeit the creative man). I turned down several full-time job offers.

When I quit, I had a townhouse with a mortgage, a horse named Fable and a dog named Turbo. That wasn't complicated enough for me, so I adopted a puppy and named her Dalia. I clearly needed a dog for each arm, Turbo on one side and Dalia on the other. You might have children and/or a spouse and your decisions might impact a lot of lives. Naturally, you forget that the decision to stay in a job you hate impacts everyone.

My finances were in great shape and I made more after six months in business than I had in a year with my old salary. And I was arrogant about it. Newbie success is dangerous, because it doesn't prepare you for a future of struggles. But it did give me hope to keep going.

Year Two: I was getting more direct client work and kept telling myself that I didn't know what I was doing. Not a helpful inner dialogue, but that's what I believed. Kitchen tables still doubled as my work area, but I had stopped going to agencies to work in-house. I would only take projects I could do offsite. I made myself a beautiful logo that took hours to hand letter. I knew I'd done a great job when my friend asked if a local designer we mutually knew had done it.

The dogs and I moved in with someone I'd been dating and I started working from their kitchen table. I rented out my place and became a landlord to some recent college grads. Then I moved my horse to a fancy stable so I could have access to indoor riding. My finances were still in good shape, but I was becoming emotionally detached from money. I realized that what I had been doing was over-rated and my money was tied up in what I was "supposed" to be doing with it. The idea of a pony icon popped into my head and the sketch was so simplistic and ugly that it stayed an idea for a year. Pony Friday entered his terrible twos and learned to walk with wobbly little legs.

Year Three: The pony icon finally came to life. One night I became caught up in a creative storm and started working on making the pony icon into a graphic. He didn't materialize quickly, but he came to life with ease. My direct client work started to get more consistent, and I was feeling as though I was building the type of creative shop that I didn't want to own. I finally hired a designer to help me part-time and we started dedicating our time to what Pony Friday could be. I paid her to work on sock designs, because I wanted socks. That was the vision—socks. I hired a business coach, who turned out to be a waste of time and money so I fired him.

My dog entourage and I moved back to my townhouse as a fam-jam of three and I bought office furniture to set up in my living room so the kitchen would be clear for eating. I also got a second desk and colour printer for my new helper. My living room became Pony Friday central and my super-saver attitude about money started to shift into a you-better-start-investing-more-in-yourself approach. Like any other three-year-old, Pony Friday was forming his identity and starting to push boundaries.

Year Four: What was previously an annual salary for me I now crushed out in two months of work. Imagine getting what you used to make in a full year in two months. Yeah, too bad I was miserable because I hadn't changed the work I was doing—I was still just work-ing for others. Finding work that makes me money is easier than creating something that I actually love to do and also makes me money. I needed help, but I had no idea what kind. We relaunched ponyfriday.com and added a store section with four items: stickers, button pins and a couple of toque styles. I was still consistently doing direct client work but rarely contracting to agencies and, more importantly, I could see Pony Friday's future taking shape into something I wanted to be part of. We did our first pop-up shop—a miserable fail.

The dogs and I moved back in with the person we lived with before—we'd started dating again—but I negotiated for a room in their house to be my dedicated office space. We painted the little ten-by-twelve-foot space Pony Friday blue on two sides and black magnetic chalkboard on the others. I finally felt like I had a legitimate home-based business. I traded creative marketing services with a leadership organization to be part of an executive leadership group.

The traditional bank refused to give me a business loan but then sent me a credit card offer in the mail, which I snapped up. My townhouse was successfully rented out to new tenants for part of the year, and the other part I had to carry an empty piece of property and all the bills that go with it. Logically, this shouldn't have been an issue, since I'd been paying those bills before, but all my money was now in Pony Friday Land. It was my money, and I spent it on what I wanted.

Year Five: The people you need are going to magically appear... well, sort of. Some local design students interviewed me for their entrepreneur class and a few months later I decided to hire them both as interns. They became Designer Three and Designer Four. The bank still wouldn't give my business a loan, but my credit card limit was increased and I accepted the longer rope with which to hang myself. We added more things to the product line and focused more attention on Pony Friday and less on client work, which was great for dream-building and tough on the bank accounts. And Pony Friday started to make friends of his own, which was weird.

Year Six: Determination is a superpower that you have to practice. I was still fighting to live my life by design and every day I got closer to my ideal. I had shoulder surgery, which took me out of the game for a bit, and I'm thankful that I had as much control over my schedule as I did. I couldn't drive for a month, and putting on anything other than elastic-waist pants was a distant dream. We finally started getting our shirts sewn at a local garment factory so we weren't printing on blanks. Financially, I was bleeding and trying to find life support. I cashed out the mutual funds that I had started contributing to when I was a teenager. I also sold my older-model vehicle, to help with cash flow, and I financed a newer model. Then I finally got a small business loan from an entrepreneurial-focused bank, using my already-overleveraged personal guarantee. My credit card limit got another bump and I got an offer for a business line of credit. This stuff is free, right?!

DECIDE WHAT BEHAVING BOLDLY MEANS FOR YOU

Year Seven: This is the year I finally started to see myself as a business owner. It's not that I ever felt like an imposter—I was more of a floundering fish flopping on the beach trying to get back into the ocean. A friend of mine compared my entrepreneurial journey to growing a human and the natural phases we all go through, reminding me that you don't expect an infant to walk or a toddler to ride a bike—they simply aren't ready. The nine-to-five jail became all but forgotten. I started doing most of my work in my home office with Designer Four. Turbo died. And to maintain my double-dog-hair quota, I adopted a puppy named Dante, whose job is to create chaos and prevent us from working while Dalia barks at the squirrels. It was—and still is—a madhouse, but we've all specialized in something. I switched accountants again and finally hired bookkeepers. I had to shake off my shame and tell them all that the numbers weren't pretty—they were downright ugly. The bookkeepers came into my office to adjust accounting entries and had to ask me, "What's this revenue from? A new client?" No, I stole it from my life partner to keep the business afloat. And that's a bounced cheque and that other one was a cash injection from selling my house.

Today, I'm closer to living my life by design and rarely experience the frustration of rush hour or have to run errands at the same time that everyone else is. My social life is pretty limited so being my own best friend is key. It's the little words of encouragement from my friends, family and the Pony Friday team that keep this thing moving forward.

Spectating Lets Fear Win

When you go to school to be a doctor, you have a general idea of how much it will cost you in living expenses and tuition. You have a basic sense of the timeline and workload because so many others have travelled this path before you. When you set out to be an entrepreneur, you're walking through a thick fog, fumbling your way forward, and it's not cheap. I continue to remind myself that the tuition for entrepreneur school is high, but it will be worth it in the end as long as I don't drop out of the program. I have to see it through to the end.

And it's not clear where that end is, but I've already weathered one heck of a storm and I believe the tides are finally turning in my favour. I can feel it. I didn't just dream of what could be: I set out to do it and I can say that after seven years of trying, I'm no longer a small freelancer baby-stepping along. I'm leaping and bounding, but that distance I've already travelled was hard to see even last year.

This is not an attempt to send you on a misguided path of throwing caution to the wind. You have to decide what behaving boldly means for you. This is about challenging your life rules and pushing past long-standing barriers or mental blocks. I'm advocating for you to believe in your own ability to lead your best life and take a chance on your own dreams, whatever that means for you. Forget knowing your plan: know your purpose and keep moving in that direction.

I heard somewhere that it is okay to go into debt until the age of thirty, as long as after that you start digging your way out. The logic must be that after thirty, you're basically old, heading for retirement

and on the downward slide toward death. In my twenties this seemed sensible. I'm forty-one now, so I know this is bad advice. I've rejected it in exchange for my reality of tossing all my money into the entrepreneurial burn barrel. This might be the most senseless thing I've ever done and it's been going on for seven years. But hey, it's got to be cheaper than marriage and divorce, or at least better for you. Did I mention I was cashing out my retirement savings too? Yep, that's happening. Clearly I forgot about that stash of cash when I was dealing with all those NSFs.

Sometimes I'm doing my best and my best sucks, but if our suppliers aren't doing their best I get to fire them. We fired the factory and the garment designer and we sourced new options out of Vancouver. The garment industry in Vancouver is competitive, so we're optimistic about this decision. It felt freeing to draw a new no-bullshit line in the sand.

Tenacity Is in My Bones

When I was two, my parents took me to the local rodeo. Not that I remember this: my dad told me this story, and my memory of his memory takes place in a parking lot on the way to the country fair, my fingers about to get sticky with cotton candy.

I toddled ahead, a little walking pylon—my ginger locks getting tousled by the strong wind. Determined toddlers are the cutest, and my dad assures me that I was no exception. The golden dumpling of my father's eye, tottering around like I owned the place, dressed in my brother's hand-me-down overalls. In top gear, I strode ahead with both parents at my back. Then, a giant blow from behind: I was knocked over. Who would wallop a small child? I was splayed out on the ground, belly-flop style. It was the kind of fall only a young child could manage without incurring an injury. I struggled to my feet. I was furious. I spun around, only to find that no one was there. My parents weren't to blame for the incident. Nope, Mother Nature had swooped in with a quick blast of wind and dropped me. She can be cruel, but that early lesson taught me to get back up and keep fighting. While I don't directly remember any of this happening, I also don't recall a moment in my life when I wasn't ready to stand back up and fight.

Nearly four decades later, I'm not so different from the tot outstretched on the dusty asphalt. I still walk around looking like a bright pylon, and I still get mad when the "forces that be" push me down. It's about getting back up—and I want you to get back up with me.

The Stress Is Worth It

Betting on myself is worth it. In ten years, ask me if I regret this or not; right now, it might be too soon to tell. I wish I could say that I started off year eight with a new laptop and a winning lottery ticket, but I can't. My laptop had a life expectancy of five years, but it's about to turn eight. It's grinding away and wishing it had been smart enough to take a job with a retirement plan and a pension. Over seven years, I lost "everything" to this journey—my house, my cushy life at the stable, a dog, my retirement savings, my investments and some friends. I have fresh coral-coloured hair that I've dubbed "fear crusher" and a credit card that keeps getting declined. I don't regret the losses, because of what I've gained.

Forget material stuff and fickle relationships.

They're irrelevant.

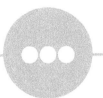

TO BE
CONTINUED

Chasing Your Dreams Is Worth It

Stay resilient. At the moment I'm going broke, which gives deeper meaning to the whole "going for broke" adage. I don't have the money to publish this book and it could very well turn out that there isn't anyone who wants to read it. But I needed to write it. It's another step on my big journey that I needed to take. I'm all in. So if going for broke and being broke are meant to be part of my path, I'm giving it a teddy-bear-worthy squeeze. Consider how much money you'd be willing to pay to avoid being miserable.

Behaving bolding isn't about flash-in-the-pan success or a guarantee of skyrocketing to greatness. You can't hire someone else to build your muscle memory. Muscle memory is the result of putting things into action. It only comes from doing a lot of tedious work—repetition, execution and improvement. It's about doing. It's about creating. It's about making. You have to be in the creative zone and hone your skills. Then it becomes about repetition. Respect yourself enough to choose your dream over money. Money will come and go—self-respect should not. Your self-respect should only grow. Hold your head high, even when you have no inkling how the winding road your intuition is driving you down will get you closer to your destination. This is about showing up for yourself; that's your purpose. The universe is dropping hints all over the place and your job is to notice the clues and run with it.

Today is another battle. Entrepreneurship is a game of patience and endurance. This is not a sprint. I'm in it for the long haul. I'm not done. I'm doing. I'll never be done. I'll always be doing and living my truth out loud. There's no happily ever after here. It's bigger than that. It's committing to living uncomfortably ever after. It's a life dedicated to dream-chasing. I'm still chasing my own tail, or at least the tail of my make-believe pony.

I'm showing up for me.

You need to show up for you.

Thank you to my parents for raising me to be myself.

Elise Russell is a quick-witted creative director known for her twisted sense of humour, attention to detail and sass. Her work has been recognized by many of the world's top advertising award shows, including the most coveted three: Cannes, D&AD and The One Show.

Often called candid, blunt and ballsy, Elise is a woman of action who prefers a cut-to-the-chase approach. She has no patience for unnecessary meetings or people who talk in circles, so she told traditional agency life to take a hike and launched Pony Friday: a hybrid creative boutique and motivational lifestyle brand. She currently lives in Calgary with her human companion and four-legged shedding machines.

Kiss My Pony App

Life as a creative entrepreneur is isolating. It feels like the only help available are traditional business coaches or mastermind groups, which are expensive and celebrate predictable thinking. You deserve a place that encourages you to trust your own instincts.

Join a community designed for full-time creative entrepreneurs to share and support each other as we grow our dreams.

Download the Kiss My Pony app today.

Printed in the USA
CPSIA information can be obtained
at www.ICGtesting.com
JSHW080205160324
59106JS00001B/4